The Boston Handbook

by John Powers
Illustrated by Peter Wallace

On Cape Publications

Cape Cod, Massachusetts
www.oncapepublications.com

ISBN-10: 0-9758502-7-X
ISBN-13: 978-0-9758502-7-5
This is the third edition of the *Boston Handbook*.
The first edition was published in 1999 by Covered Bridge Press, North Attleborough, Massachusetts.
This book was assigned the ISBN 0-58066-023-1 by Covered Bridge Press in 1999.

On Cape Publications
P.O. Box 218
Yarmouth Port, MA 02675
bostonhandbook@oncapepublications.com

To order additional copies:
www.oncapepublications.com

Contents

Acknowledgments

Most of the text herein came from half a century of living in this peculiar city on a hill. But I also am indebted to the *Boston Globe* for permitting me to dip into stories I've written for its pages and to readers who've offered suggestions and corrections. I also owe sincere thanks to Chuck Durang of Covered Bridge Press, who suggested the idea of a sequel to *The Boston Dictionary*, and to Adam Gamble of On Cape Publications, who has liberated and updated the original version of the Handbook. And, of course, gratitude is due Peter Wallace, whose illustrations belong in the Em Eff Ay.

Introduction

This town of Boston is become almost a Hell upon earth, a City full of Lies and Murders and Blasphemies; a dismal Picture and an Emblem of Hell. Satan seems to take a strange possession of it.
—Cotton Mather

Okay, we still Lie and Murder and Blaspheme. There's no joy on Joy Street, despite what the sign says. We kill our food by plunging it into hot wotta until the vitamins vanish. And we curse the chowdahedz who promised us that the Big Dig would be finished before the Sox won the Series. But we got rid of Satan a long time ago. He's living in a rent-controlled prewar slum in Noo Yawk.

We'll admit that this town of Bawstin is no Paradise. Our weather can be a bit whimsical. Our geography is somewhat cockeyed. (Why is East Boston north of South Boston?) Our driving may verge on the impromptu. But the alternative is moving to Kansas or someplace. So we aren't leaving unless we can take the Hancock Tower, the Mayah, and a bucket of steemiz with us.

We used to think that people who weren't bon heah were dazed and bewildered by our city because they couldn't tok the tok. So Peter Wallace and I dreamed up the *Boston Dictionary* a few years ago so that Bee Yew freshmen and other tourists would know that khakis aren't pants. (They're what you staht the cah with.)

But we still bump into folks who don't know that 128, 95, and 93 are all the same road, who expect ice cream in a milk shake, and who think that Evacuation Day is when the college kids move out. So we concluded that they needed the *Boston Handbook* to understand the kulcha—our amusing assortment of customs, oddities, rituals, quirks, and taboos, which caused the Reverend Mathah to wring his hands and rend his garments back in the 17th century. And he was one of us.

In the *Handbook,* we'll explain the difference between yiz and yoz, and why there's no "r" in Hahvid. We'll get you oriented about wayuh we ah, so you don't blow the weekend trying to find the West End. We'll point out where the Custom House is (It's not on Custom House Street) and tell you how to distinguish among Adams Street, Adams Street, and Adams Street. We'll give you directions to the Hyatt Regency. ("Go down past the old Jordan's and take a left where Raymond's used to be.")

If you're driving (what are you, retahded?), we'll direct you to MIT (take the Harvard Bridge), tell you how to get in and out of a rotary alive, and show you how to double-pahk the cah (leave the motor running and the right blinker on). If you're taking the T, God help you—and give Chahlie that nickel when you find him. If you're on foot, wait for the DON'T WALK sign to start flashing before crossing (assuming that you even use the crosswalk).

We'll deconstruct our cuisine for you—how to make a frappe, how to boil zucchini, how to get scrod. We'll teach you how to predict our wetha from how the wind is blowing and what you'll need to get through a blizzid. We'll explain why our new State House was built in 1795 and where to find the Darth Vader building.

We'll clear up the mystery about why the State House and City Hall are closed on June 17th. (It's Bunker Hill Day.) We'll spell out the Em Eff Ay and the Bee Ess Oh for you. We'll introduce you to Red and Raybo and Rawjuh, and match names with numbiz. We'll fill you in on the history—like the Great Molasses Flood—that most textbooks leave out. And we'll explain to you how we know when yiz ahnt from heah—you call it Beantown.

—JOHN POWERS

The Boston Handbook

How we get around

We say the cows laid out Boston. Well, there are worse surveyors.
—Ralph Waldo Emerson

The thing is, the cows were only trying to get to the Common, where they grazed among the Quakers hanging from trees. They weren't trying to get from Hyde Park to Allston in the middle of a Saturday.

Forget about pahking the cah. You can't even drive around this town. A man left Readville for Charlestown one June morning to celebrate Bunker Hill Day. He's still idling on Causeway Street, stuck behind a double-parked produce truck.

When a Bawstonian says you cahn't get theyah from heah, what he means is: Not in your lifetime. Certainly not by cah. We like to say Bawstin is a fabulous walking city. The truth is, it's a walking city by default.

1646: A CREW LAYING OUT THE FIRST STREETS OF BOSTON RUNS INTO TROUBLE...

STOP! STOP! PRESERVE THIS UNSPOILED GREENSPACE!

(The streets) are so twistified that it's as much as a common sized body can do to keep both feet in the same street at the same time.
—William T. Thompson

Our cow paths meander and baffle: Milk never quite turns into Water. They change midway through: Court abruptly becomes State. They answer to two names: Fleet Street is also Tony DeMarco Way. They leave off and resume...where? Who can say?

Confusion is chronic in a town where the Back Bay is not water but landfill. Why is Park Street nowhere near Park Plaza? Why can't you drive all the way down Washington Street? Why is Charles Street one way, then the other way? Why isn't the Custom House on Custom House Street? (It's on State.) Where's Pawl Reveah's house?

Don't ask us. We live here. We assume you've already been here once you arrive here. So we can't tell you how to get to Purchase Street, where Sam Adams used to live before he was a beer. Of if we can, you can't go that way. Not since the Big Dig, anyway.

The Big Dig turned downtown into a funhouse maze of Jersey barriers, chain-link fences, hairpin detours, truncated sidewalks, eviscerated streets, and traffic cops directing you away from where you want to go. Atlantic Avenue was split in two, its signs posted by P. T. Barnum. Go north for 93 South. Take a right to go left. The sign says:

STATE STREET CLOSED. USE MILK STREET.

Okay, where the hell is Milk Street?

On a stanchion holding up the Ahdery, the handbill says:

REPENT NOW. JESUS IS COMING BACK SOON.

Not if he was coming via Atlantic Avenue, he wasn't.

It's not as if everything was findable before the Dig, of course. We've been confusing visitors for a few hundred years. That's why the redcoats finally left town. They kept getting lost between the North End and the South End. They kept drowning in the East End, which is under wotta.

On the corner of India and Milk, a pole has arrows pointing in five directions. The one for Downtown Crossing sends you the wrong way down a one-way street. We're a little weak on signs around here. They're either missing or we never bothered putting them up in the first place. They're confusing or contradictory. Or they're simply irrelevant, because we don't necessarily call something by its name on a sign.

Nobody calls it I-90. We don't even call it the Massachusetts Turnpike. It's the Pike. We don't call it the Fitzgerald Expressway. It's just the Expressway. And we can't tell you if it's I-95 or I-93. We never look at a map. We just know—which means we're not much good at giving directions, especially if they involve tunnels and bridges.

Most Bawstonians couldn't tell you which is the Sumner Tunnel and which is the Callahan Tunnel. We just know that one goes to Logan and the other comes back. We know which one is the Ted Williams Tunnel. We just can't find the entrance. We know it's somewhere in Southie.

We're not a whole lot better on bridges. The one with the subway is the Longfellow, but most of us call it the Salt-and-Pepper Bridge because it looks like a pair of condiment shakers. The Harvard Bridge (which doesn't go to Harvard, of course) we call the Mass Ave bridge because it's on Mass Ave. The BU Bridge (which does go to BU) is also known as the Cottage Farm Bridge.

Nobody knows what to call the Coca-Cola Bridge now that the Coca-Cola bottling plant has been torn down. Since the Weeks Bridge is for feet only, nobody ever asks us about it. And the bridge that actually does go to Harvard is the Larz Anderson.

Bawstin by the numbiz

You've probably figured out that maps aren't much use if you're driving around this town. Particularly if you're driving on numbered highways. We have this habit of assigning two or three numbers to the same road—like 95, 93, and 128.

The map will tell you that 95 comes up from Prawvidents, hangs a left at 128, and goes up into Maine. The map will tell you that 93 begins where 95 and 128 meet, hangs a left at 3, and goes up into Noo Hampsha.

The Bawstonian will tell you that 95 ends at 128, that 93 begins at the Gahden, and that 1 begins at the Tobin Bridge. The road that goes from Braintree to Gloucester is 128. Asking us where 95 begins and 93 ends just confuses us.

For several miles on 128, the signs on one side of the divider say you're on 93 North. The signs on the other side say you're on 95 North. Actually, you're going east on 93 North and west on 95 North. Once upon a time, you could be on 93 North and 128 South at the same time. The Expressway is 93. It's also 1 and 3. Memorial Drive is both 2 and 3. Aren't primary numbers simple?

The Artery

There was only one (we called it the Ahdery), and it was almost always clogged during rush owah. As in bumpadabumpa, which is what we call it when your front is touching my rear. The formal name for it was the Central Artery, and it was the section of the Expressway that ran from the South Station tunnel to the Rivah and used to cut off the North End and the waterfront from downtown. The Big Dig was all about depressing the Artery, which is what it has done to us for decades.

FORGET THE SPANDEX...

HONK HONK

RECOMMENDED SAFETY GEAR FOR HUB CYCLISTS

Easy as 1-2-3?

Okay, so we're confused by the higher numbiz. But you'd think we could get 1-2-3 straight, right? Well, they changed Route 1 on us a while back, and now we aren't sure where it is. We still have signs that say 1 on the Jamaicaway, but they're just there for old times' sake. Route 1 comes up from Foxborough, where the Patriots play. Nobody is sure what happens to it after that. Some people think it continues along the Automile, through Dedham, and into West Roxbury. Others think it becomes 95, then 93, then 3, then 1 again after the Tobin Bridge. We have maps that tell you both things. Believe whatever you want.

Most of us will tell you that Route 2 begins somewhere around Fresh Pond and heads out, like Pawl Reveah did, to Lexington, Konkid, and points west. Maybe a dozen of us know that 2 goes all around the Public Garden, then proceeds up along Comm Ave, across the Rivah, and into Cambridge.

Route 3 is what we take up from the Cape. We think it ends somewhere downtown. We'd never guess it becomes Mem Drive.

You cahn't get theyah from heah

A Bawstonian will tell you that you cahn't get from Day Skwayah in Eastie to Day Street in JP. It's too fah and too hahd. But if you hafta:

Follow Chelsea to Visconti Road to the Sumner Tunnel to Cross to New Chardon to Cambridge to Tremont to Columbus Avenue to Centre to Day.

From West Roxbury (Centre and LaGrange) to Charlestown (Monument Skwayah):

Follow LaGrange to Washington to New Dudley to Harrison Avenue to Herald to Washington to Stuart to Charles to Beacon to Bowdoin to Cambridge to Staniford to Causeway to North Washington to Chelsea to Warren to Monument.

From Mattapan Skwayah to Oak Skwayah (Brighton):

Follow Blue Hill Avenue to Walk Hill to Hyde Park Ave to North Washington to the Arborway to the Jamaicaway to the Riverway to Park Drive to Mountfort to Comm Ave to Brighton Ave to Cambridge to Washington to Oak Skwayah.

How we drive

Okay, maybe Bawstin dryviz seem a bit impulsive, a tad impatient, a trifle unpredictable. But that's only if you come from someplace like Los Angeles, which never had cows and never gets snow. Or Noo Yawk, where all the streets run up and down and back and forth.

But this is a town, remember. Our streets are narrow. They come out of the Commin and run into the Hahbuh. We have rotaries and "private ways" and dead-end streets. We get blizzids and wintry mixes and shahwa activity.

So our driving isn't insane. It's merely evolved. We know where we're going, even if you don't. And we know how to get there. We don't have rules as much as customs, which over time have taken on the force of law.

Our unwritten rules of the road

- The travel lane is the left lane. The passing lane is the breakdown lane.
- To pass, tailgate until touching (i.e., bumpadabumpa), flash lights, honk horn.
- Left turn from right lane; right turn from left lane.
- Right turn on red except for when the sign says NO RIGHT ON RED. Then, take a right after slowing down.
- Speed up for pedestrians in crosswalk.
- Cutting off rival drivers is permissible if using blinker.

Bawstin driving customs

STOP SIGN

What the book says: Come to a complete halt, then proceed cautiously.

What the Bawstonian does: Slows to 10 miles an hour.

YELLOW LIGHT

What the book says: Stop if it is safe to do so.

What the Bawstonian does: Speeds up to avoid running red light or getting rear-ended.

FOLLOWING A FIRE TRUCK

What the book says: Keep back 300 feet.

What the Bawstonian does: Closes to within 30 feet, increases speed to 55 miles an hour, and drafts NASCAR-style.

DOUBLE PARKING

What the book says: Forbidden.

What the Bawstonian does: Leaves motor running and radio blaring to indicate brief errand.

YIELD SIGN

What the book says: Stop, unless you can enter the intersection safely without interfering with other traffic.

What the Bawstonian does: Speeds up while honking horn.

FEAR AND LOATHING ON NEWBURY ST...

Pahk yaw cah? Hah!

Unless you were bon heah, you cahn't pahk heah. That's what the resident parking stickers are about. That's why we have all those

DON'T EVEN THINK OF PAHKING HEAH

signs. That's why we block out the spaces in front of our homes with barrels and chairs, even though the Mayah says we cahn't. And when we're not in our naybahood, we don't pahk our cahs. We just leave them teetering on the sidewalk, hahf-awn, hahf-awf.

We leave them double-pahked with the motor running, especially on Boylston Street, to indicate we won't be long. We leave them in handicapped spaces unless there's a disabled driver about to pull in. We leave them in odd spots so obviously inappropriate—blocking garage entrances, in front of fire stations, in the middle lane of the Expressway—that any fool understands that we cahn't really be pahking.

And in the unlikely event that we find a legal spot, we jam the meter with a slug and tape on a BROKEN sign so we won't get a ticket. By the way, if you pahk yaw cah in Hahvid Yahd, they'll tow you to Meffa.

Around (and around) a rotary

Something else the British brought over with them. They call it a roundabout. We call it a rotary (pronounced roadaree). There are rules for driving in and around them, but of course, the rules conflict. The driver who's already in the rotary has the right of way. But since it's also an intersection, the car on the right—the entering car—has the right of way. There are no lanes in a rotary. Ergo, there are no rules. But there is a method.

The best way to get in and get out of a rotary is simply never to get in. Stay on the lunatic fringe and peel off quickly. Using your blinker is considered polite, but unnecessary.

The T

You don't hafta drive in Bawstin, of course. We were the first city in America to build a subway, which we've kept around as a museum piece. We call it the T. T as in tangled. T as in tardy.

BELIEVE IT OR NOT!

ALL TRUE!

THE CEDAR GROVE CEMETERY IN DORCHESTER IS THE ONLY ONE IN THE COUNTRY WITH A TROLLEY RUNNING THROUGH IT!

HIGH SPEED TROLLEY FROM ASHMONT TO MATTAPAN SQ.

MATTAPAN

BZZT

And did he ever return? No, he never returned, and his fate is still unlearned. He may ride forever 'neath the streets of Boston. He's the man who never returned.
—The Kingston Trio

Chahlie, bound for Jamaica Plain, is still riding that rickety trolley—and stahving. After they renamed the Scollay Square station, he couldn't remember where his wife was waiting with that sandwich. (Why wasn't she waiting with a nickel?)

We'd like to tell you that the MTA (some of us still call it that) has changed since the conductah wouldn't let Chahlie off. But it's still as bzah as ever. It doesn't run all night, like Noo Yawk's subways do. The downtown line doesn't connect to the airport line. You have to go in to go out. And you need a pocketful of silver to pay the fayuh. Only in Bawstin is a dollar bill not considered exact change.

The T passes for what we puckishly call "rapid transit" in this town. In the old joke, one Bawstonian asks another: "Should we walk? Or do we have time to take the T?" Not that this Byzantine web of trains, trolleys, and buses is slow and quirky, but if Pawl Reveah had taken the T to Lexington in 1775, we'd still be singing "God Save the Queen."

Going from City Point in Southie to Logan Airport, which is a few flaps of a crow's wing, requires three underground lines and two buses:

No. 9 bus to Broadway
Red Line to Park Street
Green Line to Government Center
Blue Line to Airport
No. 22 bus to terminal

How we get around 21

And getting from Hyde Pahk to Fenway Pahk can take you extra innings:

No. 32 bus to Forest Hills

Orange Line to Downtown Crossing

Red Line to Park Street

Green Line to Kenmore

No. 8 bus to Fenway Park

The Bawstonian's solution to all this go-in-to-go-out dizziness, especially between the Orange and Green lines, is simple: get off and hoof it. You can walk between Copley and Back Bay, between Mass Ave and Symphony, and between Ruggles and Museum.

The midnight ride of Pawl Reveah

Then: By foot from North Square to the waterfront, by rowboat to Charlestown, by horse to Lexington Center.

Now: By foot to Haymarket Station, Green Line trolley to Park Street, Red Line train to Alewife, No. 76 bus to Lexington Center.

How we walk
And then what makes it worse is the way Boston people walks. They all go dashin' along like they was gwine to die and hadn't but a few hours to settle their business.
—William T. Thompson

When we have no choice—when the roads are bumpadabumpa or the T is closed or running late (who can tell the difference?)—we wok. Sometimes, we even use the sidewalk, unless the bricks are all askew from frost heaves or DPW negligence. And if we have time—which means if it's before dawn or after midnight—we actually wait for the pedestrian signal and cross at the crosswalk.

Jaywalking, technically, is against the law in Massachusetts, but we Bawstonians understand that the law was written by people from Glosta and Birricka and the Vinyid (i.e., people not from heah). They live in places where you can play a game of whist in the center lane during rush hour and not be disturbed.

Crossing against the light (okay, jaywalking) is our local pastime. After all, it makes no sense to walk all the way to the conna when you can dash across the street. Isn't a straight line still the shortest distance between two points?

Crossing at crosswalks is decidedly inefficient. They're too crowded and the wait is too long. If everyone did it, the light cycle would have to be so long that it would inconvenience the drivers. So we leave the whole thing to Darwin. The race is to the swift.

How we know yiz ahnt from heah
- You drive a truck on Storrow Drive—and rip off the roof trying to get through an underpass.
- You cross at a crosswalk.
- You park your car in Harvard Yard.
- You take the T from Logan.
- You stop in the middle of a rotary.

Wayuh we ah

Crush up a sheet of letter-paper in your hand, throw it down, stamp it flat and that is a map of old Boston.
—Walt Whitman

South Boston is east of the South End. East Boston is north of South Boston. The North End is southwest of East Boston. West Roxbury isn't near Roxbury. The East End is the hahbuh. The West End doesn't exist. Got that?

The first thing you have to know about Bawstin is that it isn't Noo Yawk. Noo Yawk's shape hasn't changed since Peter Minuit forked over his mirrors and beads to the Indians. It's still an island shaped like a carrot. Boston used to be shaped like a steamed clam. It was a bulging peninsula dangling from the mainland by a neck, with three hills sticking up out of it.

That's what the Puritans liked about the place. It was easy to find, and nobody but an old crank named Blackstone lived there. "Being a necke and bare of wood, it is free from the three great annoyances of Woolves, Rattle-snakes and Musketoes," William Wood wrote to wannabe Americans back in England.

The only problem with Boston was that there wasn't enough of it. So they knocked down two of the three hills (yes, Beacon is the one that remains) and pushed the dirt into the water. That's what we call Boston Proper, which is where the Proper Bostonians lived.

These days, Boston seems to mean anything north of Providence, east of Worcester, south of Manchester and west of the Azores. "My son-in-law is from Boston," a stranger will tell us, standing in line at the Epcot Center.

"Wayuh in Bawstin?" we'll ask. "Lunenberg," he'll say. Lunenberg might as well be Kansas. If you can't get there on the T, it ain't Boston. And when we ask you "wayuh in Bawstin?" we mean which paht. Eastie? Southie? Rozzie? Dot? JP?

That's one way to pick out a Bostonian. Ask him which paht of the city he's from. A paht is a residential section made up of naybahoods. It's usually big enough to have its own high school, police station, subway stop, and city councilor. We never call a paht by its full name, if we can avoid it.

If we say:	We mean:
Southie	South Boston
Eastie	East Boston
Rozzie	Roslindale
Dot	Dorchester
JP	Jamaica Plain
the 'bury	Roxbury
Hypahk	Hyde Park

It's not enough to know which paht of Southie, though. You have to find out which naybahood. Is it City Point or the Lower End? And which paht of Dot? Codman Square? Fields Corner?

Boston is all about conniz and skwayiz. Conniz and skwayiz have a bus terminal, a smoke shop, a pizza pahlah, a packie, and a Brigham's. So there's rarely a reason for us to leave our conna or skwayah to go to someone else's. We probably couldn't find our way there anyway.

People from one paht of the city don't know much about other pahts. Try asking someone in Chahlestown how to get to Readville, which is a naybahood of Hyde Pahk. Even though the Mayah lives in Readville, nobody

The Boston Handbook

knows where it is, except that it's out by Milton or someplace.

Asking directions gets you nowhere in this town. Are you looking for Day Square in East Boston or Day Square in Brighton? Bradlee in Hyde Park? Bradlee what? Bradlee Street, Bradlee Court, Bradlee Lane, Bradlee Park, or Bradlee Terrace? There's a Cambridge Street and a Cambridge Avenue.

"How do I get to Warren Street?" someone not bon heah will inquire.

"Which one?" we'll say. "Warren Street in Roxbury? Warren Street in Charlestown? Or Warren Street in Brighton?" Not to mention the three Warren Avenues, the three Warren Squares, Warren Park, and Warren Place. They're all named after the same guy, of course. Joseph Warren, surgeon to the Sons of Liberty (Sunsalibidy), got around.

When we find a name we like, we tend to hang it all over the city. There are six Park Streets, five Adams Streets, and four Chestnut Streets. There are three A Streets, three B Streets (and a B Street Place), but only one C Street.

Dot

Saying you're from Dorchester is like saying you're from Noo Yawk. If it declared independence, Dot would be the fifth largest city in Massachusetts. So people there identify themselves by naybahood (e.g., Savin Hill, Uphams Corner, Ashmont, Neponset), by parish (St. Mark's, St. Brendan's, St. Ann's, St. Greg's), by playground (Town Field, Hemenway, Ronan Park, Franklin Field), or by all three. They wear OFD buttons (originally from Dorchester) and call the place Dotchestah. Dot, for shot.

How do we know which one you want?

There are Adams Streets in Charlestown, Dorchester, Hyde Park, Roxbury, and downtown.

There are Centre Streets in Dorchester, Jamaica Plain, Roslindale, Roxbury, and West Roxbury.

There are Church Streets in Dorchester, Hyde Park, Roslindale, West Roxbury, and downtown.

There are Franklin Streets in Allston, Charlestown, Dorchester, Hyde Park, and downtown.

There are Lincoln Streets in Allston, Brighton, Charlestown, Dorchester, and Hyde Park.

There are Mount Vernon Streets in Brighton, Charlestown, Dorchester, West Roxbury, and on Beacon Hill.

There are Park Streets in Charlestown, Dorchester, Hyde Park, West Roxbury, and on Beacon Hill.

There are School Streets in Brighton, Charlestown, Dorchester, Roxbury, and downtown.

There are Summer Streets in Charlestown, Hyde Park, South Boston, West Roxbury, and downtown.

There are Washington Streets in Brighton, Charlestown, Dorchester, and downtown. Take the wrong one, and you'll end up in Rhode Island.

There are limits to our redundancy—except for Harvard. We have four Harvard Streets, three Harvard Avenues, three Harvard Places, a Harvard Park, a Harvard Square, and a Harvard Terrace. Harvard, of course, is across the Rivah in Cambridge. And the Harvard Bridge goes to MIT. Where else would it go?

We could have called it the Massachusetts Avenue Bridge, since it's actually on Massachusetts Avenue, but that would have been obvious. Sort of like naming your main street Main Street. The idea of actually naming a street according to where it goes or what's on it went out with the Puritans.

  The Boston Handbook

What's in a name?

There is:
no beach on Beach Street
no canal on Canal Street
no school on School Street
no dock on Dock Square
no court on Court Street
no corn on Cornhill
no joy on Joy Street

Actually, there used to be a School on School Street, but we moved it to the South End, then to the Fenway. And there used to be a dock on Dock Square, until we dumped some of the hills into the harbor to make more land. But it was too much of a hassle to keep thinking up new street names, so we just left well enough alone.

That's why we still call it the Back Bay, even though we filled in that reeking cesspool during the 1860s and 1870s. It's a nice nostalgic touch, it's agreeably alliterative, and it's a bit mysterious (back of what?). It's also a useful way to tell if you weren't bon heah. No, the Lagoon in the Public Garden isn't the Back Bay.

Wayuh we ah

We still call it the West End, too, even though it vanished half a century ago. A guy with a bulldozer showed up one night and knocked it down. Jerome Rappaport still insists he didn't do it. If we ever find out who did...

Not that we're stuck in the 19th century or anything, but we don't always get around to updating our records. Some of us still say MTA when we talk about the T. When we say Government Center, we're thinking

  The Boston Handbook

Scollay Square. When we say Downtown Crossing, we mean Washington Street.

That's why we refer to vanished landmarks when we give directions. "Go down past the old Jordan's," we'll tell you, "and take a left where Raymond's used to be."

Okay, so Raymond's hasn't been there for fifty years. How are we supposed to know when you got here? Here's how we can tell.

How we know yiz ahnt from heah

- You refer to it as the Prudential Center.
- You're looking for Massachusetts Avenue.
- You say "Copely" Square.
- You pronounce it "Worchester."
- You call it Beantown.

It's The Pru. It's Mass Ave. It's Comm Ave, not Commonwealth. It's Dot Ave, not Dorchester. It's Mem Drive, not Memorial. That's why so many people from out of town end up in Summavil when they're trying to drive across the Rivah. "Take Comm Ave to Mass Ave to Mem Drive," we've told them.

We don't make it easy for vizitiz to figure out where they are. If we did, the British would still be here. Except for Southie, we don't do our streets in numerical order, like they do in Noo Yawk. And except for Southie, where Will Hunting was from, we don't use letters, like they do in Washington. That would be not only too predictable, but also damned impractical. What would you do if you wanted to put a new street between 44th and 45th or F and G? But it's not as if we don't have patterns around here. Some of our naybahoods are quite logically laid out.

Wayuh we ah

If the streets are named after:	You're in:
suburbs (Brookline, Canton, Newton, Sharon)	South End
letters (A,B,C,D)	South Boston
Revolutionary War battles	
(Saratoga, Bennington, Lexington, Trenton)	East Boston
trees (Cedar, Chestnut, Walnut, Spruce)	Beacon Hill
generals (Custer, Pershing, Lee, Jackson)	Jamaica Plain
alphabetical English noblemen	
(Arlington, Berkeley, Clarendon, Dartmouth)	Back Bay
Native American tribes	
(Cherokee, Iroquois, Pequot)	Roxbury
composers (Brahms, Haydn, Mendelssohn, Liszt)	Roslindale
poets (Longfellow, Kipling, Tennyson, Whittier)	Wellesley

A LITTLE-KNOWN PART OF BOSTON'S EMERALD NECKLACE....

THE MOODY RIVER

How we tok

And the accent!...When a real Boston man used to approach me uttering sounds like those of a brick-throated bullfrog it used to occur to me that if the Cabots really had the ear of the Almighty, He must bitterly have regretted that He ever invented the vocal organs of humanity.
—Ford Madox Ford

We speak the King's English around heah. The King was Charles, and the English was what the original Bostonians were using in East Anglia before they decided to set up housekeeping here in 1630. We still tok that way, moah aw less, even after foah hundred years of eating steemiz and conned beef, being buried by blizzids, and driving around roadarees. Queen Elizabeth understood us perfectly well when she dropped by for the Bicentennial.

We don't have an accent heah. They have an accent in Noo Yawk, where birds are boids, her is huh, and egg creams contain neither. They have an accent in Philadelphier, where nobody since Ben Franklin, a fawmah Bawstonian, has pronounced the letter "o" properly. They have an accent (or sump'n) in Jawjah. They have an accent in Eyeower, where there's an "r" in con. They even have an accent in Prawvidents, which is where we banished Rawjuh Williams in 1635 because he wouldn't stop asking for cwafee.

It's cawfee, of course. How hahd is that to say? That's one way we know yaw from Bawstin. You say hahd, not hard. You open yaw mouth and say "ah," just like the doctah says. The broad "a" and the dropped "r" are what set us apaht from everybody else. We alone can pahk the cah in Hahvid Yahd.

AR is AH

You say:	We say:	
far	fah	"Bawstin is fah from Chiner."
March	Mahch	"Sometimes, we get blizzids in Mahch."
garden	gahden	"My ahnt grows tuhmaydiz in her gahden."

OR is AW

You say:	We say:	
foreign	fawrin	"Noo Yawk is like a fawrin land to me."
orange	awrinj	"Does that awrinj come from Flawridder?"
storm	stawm	"The Cape got hammid from that stawm."

 The Boston Handbook

A (at end) is ER

You say:	We say:	
Cuba	Cuber	"Havanner is the capital of Cuber."
parka	pahker	"I bought that pahker mahked down."
pizza	peetser	"Odda me a peetser with sawsidge and unyinz."

PEETSER

The Bawstin Alphabet

A B C D E F G H I J K L M N O P Q   S T U V W X Y Z
R

ER (at end) is A (or UH)

You say:	We say:	
barber	bahbuh	"How much does yaw bahbuh chahge?"
ginger	jinja	"Want that VO with jinja aw wotta?"
order	odda	"Can I take yiz odda?"

O (at beginning) is AW

You say:	We say:	
office	awfis	"Ahl be ahta the awfis on Mahtin Lootha King Day."
or	aw	"Paypuh aw plastic?"
off	awf	"Didja turn awf the wotta faw the wintah?"

TT (in middle) is DD

You say:	*We say:*	
better	bedda	"Take a cold shahwa, and you'll feel bedda."
letter	ledda	"My muthuh got a ledda from the Guvnah."
bottle	boddle	"Empty beah boddles ah worth a nickle."

MAYAH MANEENO
CITY HALL PLAZER
BAWSTIN, MA

LEDDA

ARD is ID

You say:	*We say:*	
blizzard	blizzid	"Yewtarr has snowstawms. Bawstin has blizzids."
cupboard	cubbid	"I put the shugah back in the cubbid."
Harvard	Hahvid	"Hahvid is that chahm school across the Rivah."

ERS is IZ

You say:	We say:	
drivers	dryviz	"Bawstin dryviz ah bzah."
flowers	flahwiz	"When I said flahwiz, I didn't mean awkids."
towers	tahwiz	"My nayba just moved to Hahbuh Tahwiz."

ON (at end) is IN

You say:	We say:	
common	cawmin	"The State House is awn toppa the Cawmin."
onion	unyin	"Want unyin in that sallid?"
sermon	sermin	"The Cahdnal gave an awsum sermin on Sundee."

Local utterances

Yaw up heah rom Alabamer. Somebody in Quinzee Mahkit said you tok wikkid bzah. Does that mean yaw retahded? Not necessarily. We just find your form of dictation an amusing novelty. As faw owiz:

"bzah" means odd, in a baffling way: "The most bzah thing happened to me in Hahvid Skwayah yestiddy."

"hahf-ahst" means incomplete or sloppy: "That's the most hahf-ahst pahking job ahv evah seen."

"kweeuh" means absurd: "That paypuh we hadda write on *Silas Mahnuh* was so kweeuh."

"pissah" means excellent: "Peeuh Foah has pissah popoviz."

"retahded" means stupidly silly: "You look retahded in that pullovah swetta."

"wikkid" means extremely: "I was wikkid ty-ud after doing the Wok Faw Hunguh."

 The Boston Handbook

How We Tok

When we say: We mean:

bah   *where we drink*

"Thank Gawd the train to Noo Yawk has a bah cah."

buddha   *dairy product*

"I like my steemiz with dron buddha."

con   *what comes on a cob*

"I buy my native con out in Konkid."

khakis   *what we start the car with*

"If you lose yaw khakis again, you'll hafta take the T."

mottle   *not venial*

"Selling Babe Ruth to the Yankees was a mottle sin."

otter   *should*

"Yiz otter visit the Vaddikin when yaw in Rome."

pasta   *the parish rector*

"The new pasta at Saykrid Haht was the old pasta at Ahch Street."

shot   *not tall*

"Everybody said Tiny Ahchibald was too shot faw the NBA."

summa   *between spring and fall*

"Nanner is going down the Cape faw the summa. Chattum, I think."

tuner   *the fish*

"Ahl take the tuner on dahk, please."

wok   *what we do on foot*

"Don't wok from Bee Cee to Bee Yew. It's too fah."

The vertical pronoun: When I isn't

When we use a first-person contraction, we say "ah."

ahd = I would:

"Ahd goda the Sawx game, but ahl be down the Cape."

ahl = I will:

"Ahl have conned beef and cabbidge and a Hahp Lahguh."

ahm = I am:

"Ahm 22, and I still get cahded at the packie."

ahv = I have:

"Ahv nevuh seen a bedda pitcha than Rawjuh."

The second person: On "you" and "yoz"

If y'all are from the South (meaning anywhere below Hahtfid), you're probably baffled by what we do about the second person.

You, of course, is you by yourself. ("Can you tell me when the bus for Wistah leaves?")

Yiz is more than one of you. ("Ah yiz looking faw Sawx tickets? Ahv got three in the bleachiz.")

Awlayiz is the whole bunch of yiz. ("I cahn't take awlayiz. Ahv only got a Toyoter.")

Yoz belongs to you. ("Is this skahlit pahker yoz?")

Yaw is what you are. ("Yaw an owah late faw dinnah.")

Hahduh and hahduh

Hahduh means more difficult: "Dryvin from Rozzie ta Eastie is hahduh than I thought." It also means how to: "Can you tell me hahduh find Dot Ave?"

Bon heah—aw not?

Can't tell if someone's from Bawstin? Have her say the following dead giveaways:

"My aunt takes her bath at half-past four." (My ahnt takes her bahth at hah-pahst foah.)

"Nomar Garciaparra used to play shortstop for the Sox." (Nomah Gahshuhpahrah yoosta play shotstawp faw the Sawx.)

"Is room 444 on the fourth or the 44th floor?" (Is room foah fotty foah on the fowith aw the fotty-fowith floah?)

How we know yiz ahnt from heah

- You have an accent.
- You say the "r" in a word.
- You pronounce the "i" in bizarre.
- Your "khakis" are trousers.
- You say "how to" and "used to."

BZAH

What we eat

Boston is a great tripe center.
—David McCord

We learned how to cook from the English. We shove a large chunk of beef in the oven and leave it there until there's not a drop of juice left in it. We boil root vegetables until every vitamin seeps into the pot water. Then we dump the water down the drain and mash the residue into baby food that we can eat with a spoon. Or we plop the beef in with the vegetables for a few hours and call it a Yankee pot roast.

The whole point of Bawstin cuisine is that teeth are irrelevant. Either you don't need them, because we've boiled everything down to a puree that you can sip through a straw, or they won't do any good, because we've roasted the meat into shoe leather. But at least you'll never get trichinosis in this town. No bacterium leaves the stove alive.

THE ATLANTIC SCROD

What we call it

hot dogs: Nobody calls them franks. Franks were people who lived in France during the 9th century.

Mahzbah: Mars, Milky Way, Snickers, et cetera. If Mars makes it, it's a Mahzbah.

milk shake: If there's ice cream in it, it's a frappe. (see below)

puhdaydiz: You say potatoes. Queen Elizabeth says potahtoes. We say puhdaydiz. That's why the Irish came to Boston in the first place—because they ran out of puhdaydiz. We get them from Maine and Idaho. If we could grow them in the glacial till that passes for earth here, we would. We eat reds and whites, blues and purples and golds, russets and White Roses and blisses. We have them as O'Briens and hash browns with our farmer's breakfasts. We have them for dinna and suppa. We have them boiled and roasted and French fried and shoestringed and sauteed and whipped and mashed and smashed and *au gratin* (that's oh grahtin). We bake them, split them open, and cram them full of salsa, bacon bits and cheese, broccoli and Hollandaise. We steam them in tinfoil and think we're baking them. We put them in chowda. A meal without puhdaydiz is Chinese takeout.

sub: A submarine sandwich. We've got Italian, veal pahm, meatball, sawsidge, tuner, steak-and-cheese, Bee Ell Tee, whatevah. Grinders are those three-hour exams they give across the Rivah at Hahvid. Heroes are Tom, Manny, and Larry. "With everything" means hot peppiz, too. Faw heah?

tonic: If it's fizzy and flavored, it's tonic. That means Coke, Pepsi, Sprite, Slice, ginger ale, root beer, sarsaparilla, orange, Moxie, Jolt, Dr. Pepper, 7-Up, Mountain Dew. If we mean tonic wotta, we say tonic wotta. If we mean soda, we say club soda. If we say Pop, we mean our Dad.

How We Cook
Roasting
We start everything at 550°F, then we reduce the heat to 350. Sometimes we forget, but it's not like anybody notices. Raw, rare, medium rare, medium—that's just the starting point. We roast until well after the juices have run clear. We roast until the juices have run halfway to China.

Roast beef, no jus
Place a top or bottom round or rump (or whatever—it doesn't matter) on a rack as close as possible to the heating coil. Roast 15 or 20 or 30 minutes per pound, or until center is grayish-brown. Use residue from bottom for gravy.

Boiling
The Bostonian's all-purpose cooking method for everything from pot roast to puhdaydiz to pahster. Turn the heat up high and toss it in the pot. There's no such thing as too much wotta; you can always dump the excess in the sink.

Boiled carrots
Bring four (or eight) quarts of water to a rolling boil, gradually adding four (or eight) tablespoons of salt. Add peeled and sliced carrots. Cook for at least an hour, stirring if appropriate. Drain, or use salad spinner to remove remaining moisture.

Sauteeing (see Boiling)

Sauteed zucchini a la Hub
Wash, peel, and slice four large zucchini. Boil in four quarts of water for an hour or until tender. Drain, wring-

ing out remaining moisture with both hands. Add salt to taste. Serves eight.

Frying

Except for lobsters, there's almost nothing we can't fix in a skillet. We simply cut up a stick of buddha, turn the heat up high, and add steak, eggs, fish, or a breaded cutlet. When the smoke causes the detector to shriek, we know it's time to flip the food with a spatula.

Pan-fried steak

Place skillet on high heat. Use as much butter, margarine, vegetable oil, or Crisco as necessary to cause meat to rise to the surface. When ends of steak are pointing upward, nearly forming a U, turn and cook until all traces of pink have disappeared. Serve with one or more pats of butter.

Only in Bawstin

Boston cream pie

It may be round, but it's no pie. It's a yellow layer cake with chocolate frosting and boiled cream in the middle, cut into wedges. It's served chilled, so you can't tell when we made it. Maybe last night, maybe last year. You can't push a tray through a cafeteria line without seeing it.

Cranberries

Nobody knows how we got them. They were floating on top of the bogs down the Cape when the Pilgrims arrived. We have so many of these scarlet spheres bobbing about now that we'd need a Thanksgiving every Thursday to use up half of them. So we dump the rest into muffin mix or coat them with chocolate or string them up on Christmas trees. And since the juice is too

The Boston Handbook

"taht" to drink straight, we mix it with vodka for a Cape Codder or swirl it into cranapple, cranorange, crananything blend.

Frappe

It's pronounced frapp—no acute accent over the "e," no "ay," *s'il vous plait*. It's what folks in the Midwest call a milk shake and what people in Prawvidents call a cabinet. Milk, ice cream, and syrup mixed in a blender. A float is the milk and syrup with the ice cream on top. A frappe float is a frappe with an extra scoop on top.

Harlequin

It's a blend of vanilla, chocolate, and strawberry ice cream, available in a frozen half-gallon block. Indispensable—and unavoidable—at all birthday parties involving children under ten.

Hoodsie

Vanilla or vanilla/chocolate ice cream in a cardboard cup. Peel off the cover, and eat it with a wooden spoon.

Indian pudding

Corn meal, dark molasses, milk, and butter, baked into a grainy mush and served warm with a scoop of vanilla ice cream. Nobody has made it at home since Squanto, and the canned stuff, if you can find it, is wretched. Go to Durgin Park to get it.

Parker House roll

Soft and chewy and folded over upon itself. Once upon a time, you had to eat at the Parker House hotel on Tremont Street to get one. Now, every dining-hall caterer has them by the truckload.

Getting scrod, et cetera

Yes, this is a seafood city, even if they fly most of the swordfish up from Chile. Legal Sea Foods is our piscatorial Vatican. Here's what we're most likely to put in front of you:

Chowda

Some of us grew up singing a song called "Who Threw the Overalls in Mrs. Murphy's Chowder?" We keep it simple in Boston—milk, butter, seasonings, a little salt pork, and whatever seafood we have around. If it's clams, we're talking quahaugs (pronounced co-hogs) as big and chewy as Jason Varitek's mitt, chopped up. If it's fish, it's cod or haddock, or the catch of the day. If it's corn, we usually eat it out of a can. Light on the uny-inz and puhdaydiz, please. And only a chowdahead from Noo Yawk would throw in tuhmaydiz.

Lobster

The Puritans served it to their convicts while they chowed down on squash, pumpkin, and codfish cakes. Now, it's ten dollars a pound if you buy it out of the tank and "market price" if you get it in a restaurant. We eat it stuffed and baked, broiled, fried, and in a pie. We chop up the meat and have it in stews and bisques or mix it with mayonnaise and jam it into a hot dog roll. We plunk it down next to a filet for "surf-and-turf." We have it in milk-and-butter-and-booze sauces like thermidor and newburg. We have it lazy-man style, which means that somebody else gets to crack it open for us. We have it in the rough, which means that somebody dumps it in our lap with a couple of Handi-wipes. Don't throw away the tomalley, the gross greenish-gray slime in the middle. It's the best paht.

Scrod

Yeah, yeah, we know. I got scrod, you got scrod, we all got scrod. Except that scrod doesn't exist. It's cod, or whatever the guy behind the counter says it is. By the time we've covered it in bread crumbs and broiled or fried it to infinity, you couldn't tell the difference anyway.

Steamers

You can steam any clam that you can dig out of the muck—quahaugs, cherrystones, littlenecks, top necks, count necks, razors, gapers, geoducks, jackknifes, Manilas, mahoganies, chowder clams, sea clams, hard clams, surf clams, butter clams. But we're talking about "steemiz"— the soft-shelled clams that you steam open, dip in the scalding broth to wash off the sand, then dunk in "dron buddha" (melted butter). Don't eat the dead ones. And remember to peel off the gritty grey jacket from the neck.

You don't know beans? Neither do we.

We have them for breakfast. We serve them with hot dogs. We eat them with fishcakes. We have ham-and-bean suppers. Baked beans and brown bread has been Boston's sacramental Saturday-night repast for centuries. We have two recipes for Boston baked beans—original and modern.

Boston baked beans
Original

Wash two pounds pea beans and cover with two quarts water.

Boil for two minutes, then let soak for at least an hour.

Simmer beans until the skins burst, then drain, keeping the cooked water.

Cover half a pound of salt pork with boiling water and let stand for a couple of minutes. Drain, then score the rind with a knife.

Put the beans and pork into the pot, leaving only the rind showing. Add two cups chopped onions.

Blend one cup molasses, two tablespoons brown sugar, one tablespoon salt, one teaspoon dry mustard and add to pot.

Boil one cup of the cooked water, pour into the pot and add enough extra water to cover the beans.

Cover the bean pot and bake six to eight hours at 250 degrees. Add water as needed to keep the beans from drying out. Uncover for the last hour of baking to make the surface crisp.

Modern

Open two cans of B&M Baked Beans. Heat in large saucepan over medium temperature for ten minutes.

Boston brown bread

Original

Mix one-half cup rye meal, one-half cup yellow corn meal, one-half cup whole wheat flour, one teaspoon baking soda, one-half teaspoon salt.

Stir in three-eighths of a cup molasses and one cup buttermilk. Add one-half cup chopped seedless raisins.

Blend thoroughly and place into two small greased molds or a larger loaf pan.

Cover, put on a rack in a Dutch oven or deep kettle and add boiling water to halfway up around the mold. Steam for two hours in small molds or three in loaf pan. Keep water boiling, adding more as needed to maintain level.

Remove molds from water, uncover and heat in a 300-degree oven for 15 minutes. Let cool for 20 minutes and remove the bread when inserted toothpick comes out clean.

Modern

Open both ends of can of B&M Brown Bread (with raisins, if desired). Push bread out of empty can and wrap with aluminum foil. Heat in a 300-degree oven for 25 minutes.

Dinner? Supper?

Same thing. Depends on the day. On Sundays and major holidays, we have dinner instead of lunch, but it looks like supper. A roast, puhdaydiz, all that. We even say grace. Supper is what we have during the week.

What we drink

Beah, wine, and hahd stuff. We can't get any of it at supermarkets, so we have to go to the packie, which is short for package store. That's what the Puritans did to us—we can't call it a liquor store. We have to pretend it's cider that they're putting in those brown paper bags. If you don't look old enough, you get cahdid—asked for your driver's license or another photo ID. That's why everyone under 21 in this state comes from Maryland.

Eating out

Boston is a terrific restaurant town now, ever since Immigration let people come in from places other than Sicily and County Cork. You can get Szechuan, Thai, Ethiopian, Tuscan, Jamaican, Vietnamese, Portuguese, Peruvian, French-Cambodian, Russian, Afghan, Salvadoran. But the Bostonian still goes where his father did—Jimmy's, the No Name, and the Union Oyster House for fish; Joe Tecce's for Italian; Jake Wirth's for German; the Hilltop in Saugus for steaks; and Locke-Ober and Pier Four, if someone else is paying. The quality of the cuisine is irrelevant; quantity is everything. If we have to loosen our belts and ask for a doggie bag, we're in ecstasy.

How we know yiz ahnt from heah

- You order a grinder and a soda.
- You ask for the Boston cream pie *á la mode*.
- You expect ice cream in a milk shake.
- You wear a t-shirt that says: "I got scrod at Legal Sea Foods."
- You steam your vegetables.

What we build

Clear out 800,000 people and preserve it as a museum piece.
—Frank Lloyd Wright

Okay, so we've still got Paul Revere's house. We've still got our original State House from 1713 and our original City Hall from the Civil War.

We kept the Garden for the rats to scamper around in even after we built the FleetCenter, which changes its name every week. The Garden, after all, was a splendid example of the Moderne phase of the ornamental French Art Deco school.

BOSTON'S MASTER BUILDERS

CHARLES BULFINCH

BESSIE

TOURISTS FROM BOSTON VISIT TOPEKA KANSAS

YOU ONLY HAVE ONE STATEHOUSE? BZAH!

We don't throw buildings away like used Kleenex just because they happen to be a few hundred years old. We're a classical kind of city. Rome still has its Colosseum. Athens still has the Parthenon. Paris still has Notre Dame. Why shouldn't we keep the Custom House?

And why should we knock down a perfectly good building just because we built another one by the same name nearby? Just because the odd tourist from Kansas or someplace gets confused?

"Can you tell me how to get to the State House?" he'll ask us, turning these huge maps this way and that.

"Which one?" we'll want to know.

"What do you mean, which one?" he'll ask, bewildered.

"The old one or the new one?" we'll reply.

"You mean, you've got two of them?" he'll say.

Kansas hasn't been around long enough to have two State Houses. When George Washington was riding his white charger along Cornhill to our first one, the Pawnee were still playing hide-and-seek among the corn fields.

But we've been here long enough to have two of practically everything. We've even developed a foolproof way of telling them apart. We call one the Old Whatever and the other the New Whatever. Maybe in a late-model city like Phoenix or Las Vegas, it seems strange that our New State House was built in 1795, but there you are.

We just didn't see any good reason for tearing down the Old State House, because it wasn't that old in the first place. Even now that a couple of hundred years have gone by, the old version still works fine. The windows open and close, the roof doesn't leak, and the statues of the lion and the unicorn still look nifty. When Chicago wanted to buy the building a while back and move it out there, we said nix. We still needed it for a subway entrance.

A FAILED PRESERVATION ATTEMPT.....

Stop the Big Dig

SAVE THE HISTORIC CENTRAL ARTERY

Their buildings, like their women, are neat and handsome.

—London Spy (1699)

It's not true that Charles Bulfinch built our whole city, but he did build most of it—or at least most of what we kept around. He was a Federalist kind of guy, and he worked mostly in brick and granite. That's what gives Boston its quaint look. We're a masonry city. Want to make something out of it?

The thing about brick and granite is that they look classic and dignified for centuries at a time. And they don't burn much, unless you put a wooden roof on top and soak it down with tar.

That's the lesson we learned from the Great Fire, which burned down 700 buildings (give or take) that we assumed were fireproof. We had forgotten that we'd carved out the granite from the bottom of the Quincy quarries. When the water in the stone heated up, everything blew halfway to New Hampshire.

Still, we're big fans of masonry because it's easy to work with, it weathers well, and it stays up forever. That's why we have so much stuff left over from the 1800s. It'd be a crime against aesthetics to rip down a courthouse just because the clock stopped working or we ran out of shelf space.

So we just build a duplicate, and everybody's happy. It's an architectural twin spin. We'll admit, sometimes the nomenclature can be a tad misleading. You'd think if we have an Old North Church, that we'd have a New North Church somewhere. Nope. And that if we had an Old South Meeting House, there'd also be a New South Meeting House, right? Nope.

We call them Old North and Old South because they're so old it's as if they've been here forever. Like

Old Ironsides. It's our affectionate way of referring to our colonial heritage. They're places that are so unique, so eternal that they're not only irreplaceable, they're inimitable. Nobody would dare build a New Ironsides. So we didn't.

The fact is, we don't build anything new until we absolutely have to. Like the Gahden. It was practically falling down. The lights kept burning out, the compressors kept blowing up, and it smelled like elephants half the time. They even found a dead monkey in a circus jacket up in the rafters. But we couldn't bear to knock the historic old heap into rubble. "There'll be a Polish pope before we build a new arena," we vowed.

FROM THE VAULTS OF THE BRA
SOME PROJECTS WE *DIDN'T* BUILD....

NEW IRONSIDES

FRANK LLOYD WRIGHT'S PROPOSED REHAB OF PAUL REVERE'S HOUSE

ONE THERMOS PLACE

Anyway, you should see what we *haven't* built in this town. Like the Wurlitzer. Like Stonehenge. Like Thermos City. Those were some developer's big idea of modern architecture in the 1980s. If you go down to City Hall and rummage around in the BRA's closets, you'll find the scale models still gathering dust.

The Wurlitzer was 41 stories of pewter-toned aluminum and blue-tinted glass that was shaped like a 1947 jukebox. Somebody wanted to plug it into Fort Hill, but we couldn't figure out where the quarters went.

Stonehenge was going to be a huge mini-city down on the Fan Pier, with a matched set of harborside towers that would have lured Druids from around the planet to worship. We decided we couldn't handle the traffic jams during the summer solstice.

Thermos City was going to be plunked down where the FleetCenter finally went up. It had a 70-story tower that looked as if you could unscrew the top and start pouring. If it had come with a lunch pail, it might have worked.

If we'd built a tenth of the stuff these urban dreamers begged us to, we'd look like Houston, f'crissake. Like the flying saucer stadium they wanted to put next to South Station. Or the 500-foot ICBM missile made of limestone and glass that Doctah Silbah wanted to build at BU. We were afraid he would have launched it toward Harvard. Or Park Plaza, the "city within a city" across from the Common that would have taken ten years to build.

There's always some joker with a lawyer, a $10,000 line of credit, and an Etch-a-Sketch who blows into town and wants to build an 800-foot tower that'll cast an eternal shadow on Faneuil Hall. We point him toward Salt Lake City.

We've already got the Darth Vader building, and that's weird enough. It stands on the corner of Boylston and Exeter, this sullen sentry made of brick and dark glass that looks like the dusky-visored Lord himself, fresh from the second reel of *Star Wars*. A force in the Back Bay, the builders called it. We're still waiting for the Jedi to return with the wrecking ball.

Right around the corner, there's the Gainesburger building, a mass of mealy red brick that looks like it belongs in a dog dish. We wanted to ship it over to Wonderland, but even the greyhounds turned up their noses.

That's the problem with architecture. You can vote a bad mayor out of office (not that we do, of course). You can trade a bad shortstop to the Astros. You can't get rid of a bad building unless you can bribe someone to blow it up. You and your children and your grandchildren have to walk past it every day on your way to Quincy Market.

So we don't make it easy to play with an erector set in this town. We're big on renovation, on what architects call "adaptive re-use." If it was good enough for Charlie Bulfinch, it's still good enough for us. Just strip the floors, paint the trim, and wash the windows. Frank Lloyd Wright can look down his prairie-style nose at our Federalist museum pieces here. We'll toss a brick right through his picture window. Most folks around here think he's Wilbur and Orville's kid brother anyway.

How we know yiz ahnt from heah
- You can't find the New Garden.
- You're surprised that the New State House is 200 years old.
- You confuse Bulfinch with the Bull & Finch.
- You don't know which City Hall contains the Mayah.
- You've never heard of Park Plaza.

Us, parochial?

Why should I go anywhere? I'm already here.
—a Boston matron, circa 1880

Boston is the Hub of the Universe. Okay, so a Bostonian said that. Actually, Oliver Wendell Holmes declared that the State House was the sub of the solar system, and we've been blissfully misquoting him for 150 years or so. But nobody we know disagrees.

The thing about hubs is that everything revolves around them, and they don't go anywhere. That's why we stay right on our own conna and don't go anyplace we don't have to. Because if enough of us venture beyond Route 128, the whole cosmos might spin off and vanish down a black hole. That's what somebody at MIT told us, and MIT is the finest technological institute on the planet. If it weren't, it wouldn't be here. Since it is here, why go anywhere else?

ONE DAY IN ROZZIE...

IT IS AN HONOR TO BE HERE IN THE HUB OF THE UNIVERSE AND TO MEET A HIGHER BEING LIKE YOURSELF!

THIS IS WIKKID BZAH!

The Bostonian who leaves Boston ought to be condemned to permanent exile.
—William Dean Howells

When people from the other five or six world-class cities tell us we're parochial, we scratch our heads. In Boston, parochial means Catholic. And the dictionary says that catholic means universal. So we don't know what the hell they're talking about.

Provincial? Okay, maybe we are provincial. We talk as if what we have is the only one of its kind. It isn't Boston Harbor. It's The Harbor. It isn't Boston Latin. It's The Latin School. It isn't the Charles River. It's the River. If anybody else has one, we probably had ours first.

Maybe somebody else does have a Latin school or a harbor. We know about what occurs elsewhere mostly by rumor, and only if it happens to involve a Bostonian. A typical *Globe* headline would be:

HUB MAN DIES IN WASHINGTON DC NUCLEAR HOLOCAUST

If the Hub man were someone prominent, like the Guvnah or the Mayah or the Cahdnal, then it would be page-one news.

Even our holidays are provincial. Everybody else says that March 17th is St. Patrick's Day. In Boston, it's Evacuation Day. That's when we dragged a bunch of cannons to the top of Dorchester Heights in 1776 and pointed them at the British ships that were sitting in the harbor. So the redcoats thought it might be a good idea to head for Trenton or someplace.

Everywhere else, June 17th is merely June 17th. Here, it's Bunker Hill Day. We celebrate a battle that we lost to the British and that actually took place on Breed's Hill.

But it was our battle and our hill and who cares what they think in Oklahoma? Oklahoma celebrates Cherokee Strip Day. Here, it's just September 16th.

The morals of our people are much better; their manners are more polite and agreeable; they are purer English; our language is better; our taste is better; our persons are handsomer; our spirit is greater; our laws are wiser; our religion is superior.
—John Adams

We've been a world-class city since John Winthrop brought his picnic basket ashore in 1630. Nobody has to tell us. We just know. The Celtics have won 16 world championships—it says so right on all those green-and-white banners. Our newspaper is called the *Globe*. We have the greatest university in the world, the greatest high school, the greatest library, the greatest hospital, the greatest restaurant, the greatest subway, the greatest symphony, the greatest museum.

When we say greatest, of course, we mean oldest. The words are interchangeable. Boston Latin goes back to 1635. Harvard goes back to 1636. The library was founded in 1854, the subway was opened in 1905, the BSO in 1881. In 1881, they were still living in log cabins and hunting buffalo with bows and arrows in Colorado. Denver won't be a world-class city until 2200, at the earliest.

The older—and, therefore, greater—something is in Boston, the more reluctant we are to change it. Like the old Garden, where the Bruins and Celtics played forever.

It was a grimy wreck of a playpen with no escalators and no air conditioning. The corridors were narrow, and the seats were uncomfortable, and King Rat

The Boston Handbook

and his progeny had the run of the place. The compressors were so old that the Broons would be skating in the fog in the springtime. They actually had a hockey game called on account of darkness when a transformer blew and the lights went out.

But we loved the Garden because it was so damned old that there was no other place like it. The Seltz won a world championship one year because a weekend heat wave turned the place into a sauna and the climate-controlled Lakers got so dehydrated that they couldn't run anymore.

We hung on to the Garden until the wrecking ball knocked the roof in. We insisted on calling the Fleet-Center the New Garden until the TD Banknorth folks acknowledged the inevitable and brought back the name. And for old times' sake, the Celtics kept using their old parquet floor, with all the dead spots in it.

Us, parochial? 67

TEARING DOWN OLD BOSTON GARDEN...

Same thing with Fenway Park, which opened the same week that the Titanic went down. John Updike called it a lyric bandbox nearly half a century ago, but we keep quoting him as if he wrote it yesterday. It's creaky and cramped now, despite the improvements, and the scoreboard in the wall (which the leftfielder uses as a urinal when he's caught short), is still kept by hand. You need a new ballpark, outsiders tell us. Babe Ruth played there, for godsake. That's why we can't tear it down, we reply. Babe Ruth played there. It's a historical landmark.

That's why we didn't build a new hotel room between 1927 and 1955. There was nothing wrong with the Ritz and the Parker House. "The people who worked on State Street sat at their rolltop desks and thought everything was all right," John Collins, the former mayor, once said. "Because it was the same today as it was yesterday."

ONE DAY AT FENWAY PARK

SO HARRY, WHAT DO YOU THINK OF THOSE NEW 'DUGOUT SEATS' INSTALLED IN WHAT USED TO BE FOUL TERRITORY?

IT'S OK WITH ME.

I'M GLAD THE NEW OWNERS ARE MAKING AN EFFORT TO EXPAND FENWAY'S EXISTING SEATING CAPACITY RATHER THAN BUILD A NEW BALLPARK.

ALTHOUGH, THOSE 'PITCHER'S MOUND' SEATS HAVE GOT TO GO!

When you eat at Durgin Park—where the food, the tablecloths, and the waitresses haven't changed since 1742—the menu tells you: Your grandfather and perhaps your great-grandfather dined with us, too. What it doesn't tell you is: And if you don't like it here, the train for Oblivion (which is a suburb of New Haven) leaves at 5:07.

We didn't care when Ben Franklin left for Philadelphia. We kicked Roger Williams out, and he ended up running Providence. The Braves went to Milwaukee in 1953, and nobody noticed for two seasons. We just thought that they were on an extended road trip.

When Jerry Jacobs, who owns the Bruins and the Garden, didn't like the deal he was getting on a new building, Tommy Finneran (then the Speaker of the House) pointed toward Arizona. "I invite him to walk," Finneran declared.

The Bruins once threatened to move to New Hampshire. We shrugged and offered to rent them a Mayflower van. When the Patriots said they were going to Hartford, we told them they'd already been gone for 26 years. Foxborough is not Boston, we reminded them.

Foxborough is practically in Rhode Island, which is halfway to New York. New York is 240 miles from the Frog Pond, which means that it takes most of your day to get there. We hear that people in Texas think nothing of piling into a car and driving 600 miles to go to the beach. In California, they'll tell you that Pasadena is "only" a three-hour drive from San Diego, like it's just around the block. If we drive anywhere for three hours, we take along bottled water, traveler's checks, and an interpreter.

This is a hell of a long way from East Boston.
—Joseph P. Kennedy, in London

Boston is a walking city. If we can't go by foot or take the T, we say the hell with it. Which means that our concept of distance is a bit condensed. Anything past 128 is prairie. We should have a billboard at the Weston tollbooths on the Pike saying:

THIS WAY TO KANSAS

And beyond 495 is _terra incognita_. We've been thinking about putting a sign there, like they had on maps in the 15th century, warning that you'll fall off the edge of the earth if you go any further.

Us, parochial? 71

Somebody once printed a map of the Bostonian's view of the world, with Nebraska and China and Russia vaguely out there beyond Comm Ave. Lots of us have it framed on our rec-room wall for reference, just in case we need to travel to those uncharted wastelands.

Hell, when we go down the Cape for a weekend, we pack as though we're with the Donner Party. Who knows if they have corkscrews in Chattum? What if we run out of Brigham's pistachio?

If we were meant to be anywhere else, we wouldn't have been bon heah. Our provincialism is mostly a matter of birth certificate. Unless you were born in Boston, you're here on a permanent green card. "I've been here since 1968," said Larry Moulter, the man who built the FleetCenter (a.k.a. The New Garden), "but to Dapper O'Neil, I'll always be the kid from Connecticut."

That's why we're so churlish about giving directions. If you're a native Bostonian, you know how to get from Dot to Rozzie. If you aren't, and you don't, what's the point in your going there?

Nothing personal. We're provincial to each other, too. People in Neponset and Savin Hill put bumper stickers on their cars that say OFD (Originally From Dorchester). Just so the social climbers from Southie know their place.

We never say we're from South Boston or Dorchester or Roxbury. That doesn't narrow it down enough. We're from Uphams Corner or City Point or Grove Hall. If you have to ask us where that is, you weren't bon heah.

All Bostonians, when they die, if they are good, go to Paris.
> **—Thomas Gold Appleton**

How we know yiz ahnt from heah
- You wonder why City Hall is closed on June 17.
- You refer to the Charles River.
- You like the New Gahden.
- You assume we know who the governor of New York is.
- You call it the Hub.

HARRY JOINS THE **L ST. BROWNIES** FOR THEIR ANNUAL NEW YEAR'S DAY DIP IN BOSTON HARBOR

Weather—or not?

Covered & foggy. Soon clear & hazy.
—John Winthrop, 1747

This isn't San Diego, where they don't even bother with weatherpersons. Who needs to pay somebody to tell you that tomorrow is going to be just like today, which was the same as yesterday? This isn't Seattle, where the sun comes out so rarely that people think it's the wake-up call for the Apocalypse. And this isn't Atlanta, where a single snowflake backs up traffic all the way to the Florida panhandle.

We have real weather here and, yes, it is contradictory. "Clear & hazy" doesn't begin to describe some of it. We have hurricanes and blizzids and nor'easters, Indian summers, May freezes, and January thaws. We have snow in October, rain in February. We have days where the mercury will drop 40 degrees between noon and midnight. We're always stowing the shovels too early and pulling out the tank tops too late. We go through a lot of Sudafed around here.

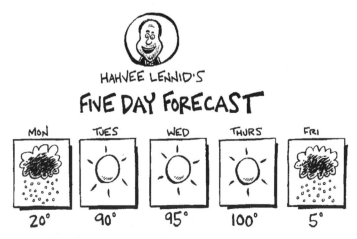

HAHVEE LENNID'S
FIVE DAY FORECAST

MON	TUES	WED	THURS	FRI
20°	90°	95°	100°	5°

Other places have climates. Boston has weather. It's inconvenient, inconsiderate, frequently intolerable. Once in a while, it's wonderful, of course, but we regard wonderful as an aberration. That's our Calvinism, you see. We expect that life will be a trial by fire and ice. We expect to have to suffer on earth in order to attain Paradise. That's why the San Diego people are going straight to Hell. It's their punishment for bodysurfing while we were shoveling.

In the Aleutians weather is a menace, in Los Angeles a monotony, in England a mistake; but in Boston it is simply a problem.
—David McCord

When folks talk about what they miss about Boston (actually, they say New England, but they're just being generic), they say it's the change of seasons. What they mean is the weather, but only a lunatic would admit that he misses the weather we have around here. Actually, we have the same seasons that everybody else does, only more so. They're just more noticeable—and unreliable.

We'll have a foot of snow on the ground on the first day of spring. Our kids are still in school on the first day of summer, sweating out the snow days that we used up in January. Nothing's close to falling on the first day of fall. And we've already had the heat on for weeks by the first day of winter.

Our seasons change whenever the hell they feel like it, and they don't worry about being whimsical. We'll have 40-degree days in May, 60-degree days in February. So we don't pay much attention to what the calendar says about solstices and equinoxes.

Spring begins on opening day in Fenway, even if there's a 20-degree wind chill and the pitchers are wearing par-

The Boston Handbook

kas. Summer starts on Memorial Day, fall on Labor Day. And winter commences as soon as the Thanksgiving high-school game is over.

Winter

Our weatherpersons (you can't call what we have here meteorology) will talk about "seasonable temperatures," as if we actually have such things in the winter. When they say that seasonable is 40 degrees, they mean it's the average of 20 and 60. That's why we're always walking around with a hacking cough and clogged sinuses, because we're never sure how to dress and we're always guessing wrong.

And, yeah, it's a geographical fact that Boston is at the same latitude as the Riviera, but they don't have our wintry mix in St. Tropez. "Wintry mix" is our charming euphemism for the icky and treacherous blend of snow, ice, sleet, slush, and freezing rain that falls from the skies when the temperature is somewhere between 30 and 35 degrees.

We can tell it's coming when we hear the word "changeover." What's in the middle during the change-over from snow to rain or rain to snow is the wintry mix. We usually get the wintry mix during the morning or evening commute. And because it's neither snow nor rain, our DPWs don't bother sanding or plowing because it might turn out to be a waste of time and taxpayers' money.

So we slog through it in our good shoes and curse and hope that there's enough tread left on the radials to keep us from sliding into the guard rail on the Pike extension after an 18-wheeler sprays filthy semifreddo all over our windshields and the wipers freeze.

We hate wintry mixes because they're so damned deceptive. If we shovel our walks and driveways and throw our backs out lifting a thousand pounds of watery slush, odds are 100 precent that it'll all turn to rain an hour later. And if we don't, it's guaranteed that the slush will turn to five inches of ice and rip out our transmission-fluid pan.

At least with snow, we know what we're getting. One-to-three. Four-to-eight. Eight-to-twelve. That's how we gauge snowstorms around here, by inch range. The weatherpersons always give themselves four inches or so of leeway and throw in a bunch of "ifs." If the wind doesn't shift. If the storm does or doesn't blow out to sea. Four along the coast, eight outside of 128.

One-to-three doesn't bother us. Four-to-eight is annoying-to-aggravating, depending on whether the stuff is heavy and wet and whether school is cancelled. Eight-to-twelve has us stocking up at the supermarket like survivalists. Milk, water, batteries, candles, bread, Pampers, beef jerky, Sterno cans, and the *National Enquirer*. Eight we can handle. Twelve is a blizzid.

There's no fixed line to tell you when a snowstorm becomes a blizzid, but it's like pornography. We know

it when we see it. And most of the time, we can hear it coming—the Accuweather guy uses the phrase "additional accumulation possible due to blowing and drifting."

"Additional accumulation" means over a foot. You can bet your felt-lined L.L. Bean boots on that. And when we think "over a foot," we think Blizzid of '78. The Blizzid of '78 is like Pearl Harbor, the Kennedy assassination, and the Sox winning the Series. We all remember where we were when it happened.

We were somewhere past Braintree on 128 around 10 p.m. when we said the hell with it, left the car in the middle lane, and began walking toward Quincy. We were watching the second game of the Beanpot and ended up sleeping with King Rat in the bowels of the Garden until Thursday. We were stuck on the four-to-midnight shift and ended up eating out of the company snack machines for three days. We were in Cleveland, and our wives were stuck with the kids and an overdrawn checking account. We were in the kitchen of our house in Hull when it got swept out to sea. Very few of us were in the Bahamas.

We've never gotten over the Blizzid of '78. We won't get over the April Fool's blizzid, either. The crocuses were already up, the Sox were about to come north, we had loaded up on marshmallow bunnies for Easter, and the Mayah had put the plows away for the season. That's why the true Bostonian leaves the storm windows up until Memorial Day. We won't get fooled again.

March

What we call a "hahf-ahst" month. It's not really winter, but for damned sure it's not spring. It's grey and raw and windy most of the time. We're sick of sitting indoors but nobody wants to be outdoors. We can't plant anything, but we can't put away the parkas and boots, either. We hear baseball on the radio, but it's coming from Florida. All that lion-and-lamb business was dreamed up somewhere else. It's the 29th of the month, Easter is five days away, the temperature is 41 degrees with 30-mile-an-hour gusts, and the heavens are spitting snowflakes.

Spring

Some years we have it, some years we don't. Sometimes, we have snow on the ground two weeks into April. Sometimes, it's 90 degrees by the last week in May. Spring is a relative term around these parts. We know it's here when the forecasters start talking about "shower activity." That means rain, enough rain to put Morrissey Boulevard under water and turn every Little League diamond into a rutted quagmire.

Now and then we get a week so glorious—65 degrees with a lilting breeze, songbirds trilling at dawn, fruit trees popping into bloom—that we kid ourselves into thinking that spring here is like it is in Virginia or Tuscany or Provence. An authentic, mark-your-calendar, three-month season. Hah!

Summer

You'd think that after putting up with wintry mixes and such that we'd get a nice, warm, breezy summer. Sunny days and cool nights. We do, of course, down the Cape. (Except when we're down there for vacation in July, when it's cloudy for four days, pours on the weekend, then brightens as soon as we come back across the Sagamore.)

Up here, as often as not, we get what they have in the Bible Belt—the three Hs. Hazy, hot, and humid. It's wet-sauna stuff that drifts up the coast from Savannah or somewhere and hangs over us for days.

We've had the three Hs around here since a few months after the glaciers receded, yet we still regard them as an unseasonable surprise. We haven't put the air conditioner in the bedroom yet, and the fans are gathering dust in the cellar. We haven't accepted that we're at the same latitude as the Riviera.

Or maybe we can't understand why we get both the wintry mix and the three Hs. The rest of the country gets tradeoffs. They sweat like hogs down in Mississippi, but they don't have to dig themselves out of blizzids. And they may be permafrosted up in Minnesota, but they're not steamheated in the summer. So why us, damn it? Why should San Diego get perfect weather? It's 75 degrees every day of the year there, and at night the Pacific wafts over a few zephyrs to cool everybody down. There are no mosquitoes, and everybody wails like banshees if the humidity creeps above 20 percent.

The Boston Handbook

That's why we'd never want to live in San Diego, we tell each other. Because every perfect day is like every other perfect day. No variety, no surprises. We'd hate that.

Fall

When we talk about the change of seasons, what we mean is fall, specifically October. The harvest has been gathered up (yes, we grow other things besides cranberries), the pumpkins are sitting in piles, the leaves are turning orange and scarlet and gold, the earth smells rich and loamy, the air has a tang to it, and Saturdays are for football.

We invented football here, you know. That Princeton-Rutgers thing was really a soccer game. Football happened in 1874 when a bored Harvard guy picked up the ball and ran with it. Ninety years later, we had the Super Bowl.

Sometimes, we get Indian summer in the middle of fall. Nobody's exactly sure where the term comes from or why the Indians had different summers from everybody else's. But sometime in October, after we've put our Bermudas into winter storage and the Sox are watching the Series on TV like the rest of us, we'll get a couple of 70-degree days and tell each other that it's Indian summer.

All this change-of-seasons business, of course, leaves out hurricanes. We hear about them as soon as they start whirling across from Africa, but we don't pay much attention until they've been upgraded from a tropical storm to the H word and have busted up a couple of Caribbean islands. If we flip on the Weather Channel and see the waves breaking over the beachside highway on Cape Hatteras and cars afloat, we start checking the larder.

The Boston Handbook

But we don't start battening down until we see a TV talking head standing on the beach in a rain hat with the gales blowing the words over her shoulder. Then, it's officially a hurricane.

By the time they reach us (except for the likes of Bob and Carol and a few others), they've usually been reduced to wind and rain. Our favorite hurricanes, of course, are those that batter New York, then head harmlessly off to Nantucket.

Wind

Maybe we're not Chicago, but this still can be a hell of a windy city. Just stand on the corner of St. James and Clarendon and watch people trying to walk past the Hancock Building.

QUIZ THIS IS A PICTURE OF:

A. HURRICANE BOB

B. A TYPICAL DAY IN FRONT OF THE JOHN HANCOCK TOWER

We are on the ocean, after all, and our weather is always either blowing out to sea or blowing in. We don't need to stick our fingers in the air to tell where the wind is coming from. We can smell it, feel it, or see it. From the:

Northeast: Two or more days of rain or snow, depending on the season. That's your Nor'easter (or, as some say, Nawtheastuh). A hateful, horrid thing. It's the ill wind that blows nobody good.

Northwest: We love it in the summer, because it pushes the three Hs off toward France. We curse it in the winter, when it gives us sub-zero wind chills. The weatherpersons call it the Alberta Clipper or the Montreal Express, because it sweeps down from Canada.

East: Cool, refreshing, with none of your precipitation. We know it by its whiff of distant fish.

Southeast: Whatever they're having down in the Carolinas, it brings up here. That means a tease of a 50-degree day in January. It also means a week of the three Hs in July.

How we know what the forecast is

Bostonians don't need Harvey Leonard (Hahvee Lennid, to us) or any other weatherman to know which way the wind is blowing. We just glance up at the Hancock Building (the old one, not the new one) and check out the color-coded tower for the forecast. As the rhyme says:

> Steady blue, clear view.
> Flashing blue, clouds due.
> Steady red, rain ahead.
> Flashing red, snow instead.

If you see flashing red in the summer, it means that the Sox home game has been called off. If the Sox are playing in Detroit, it means we're in for a blizzid.

 The Boston Handbook

How we know yiz ahnt from heah

- You think spring begins on March 20.
- You put in your air conditioner in June.
- You think Bob and Carol are the couple next door.
- You've seen a tornado up close.
- You believe the weatherman.

Ah, kulchah

That's all I claim for Boston—that it is the thinking center of the continent, and therefore of the planet.
—Oliver Wendell Holmes

They didn't call us the "Athens of America" for nothing, you know. Maybe it was we who called us that, actually. It's been a century or two, after all. But who's going to argue with us? We had the first school (Latin, 1635) and the first college (Hahvid, 1636). We had the first library (1854), the Bee Pee Ell. We have the Em Eff Ay and the Bee Ess Oh. We have the Nutcrackah. We have the Sawx. What more do we need?

That's how all the Banned in Boston business began. We already had plenty of books. We didn't need Ernest Hemingway to tell us that the sun also rises. Hell, it rises here before it rises in Chicago. We already had translated Caligula from the original. We didn't need to see the movie. And, yeah, we walked out when Brahms's *Second Symphony* was played in 1882. We'd already heard the first one.

It's not like we're these Puritan bluenoses who go around tearing pages out of novels and putting bloomers on marble statues. It's just that we aren't Albuquerque. We weren't impressed by the Impressionists. We already had John Singer Sargent.

One feels in Boston, as one feels in no other part of the States, that the intellectual movement has ceased.
—H. G. Wells

Okay, Wells was a futurist, and maybe he thought that our clocks had stopped around 1820 or so. It's just the Hub of the Universe thing again, applied to the life of the mind. We're sitting in the middle with our intellectual curiosity, and the rest of the cosmos is revolving aimlessly around us. It's like G. E. Woodberry said, "You may know a Boston man by two traits...he thinks he knows and he thinks he's right."

We've had so many books in this town for so long that we're simply awash in knowledge. When John Harvard helped the Puritans start their charm school across the Charles, he didn't give them his lower forty for the Yard or build a lecture hall. He gave them his library, most of which was about the Devil or how to grow squash in glacial till.

Harvard has 13 million books now, give or take a rare text, and it keeps buying more. The Atheneum scooped up everything that was on George Washington's nightstands from everywhere he ever slept. Even so, we still

built a huge library in Copley Square and tacked on an addition. If there's anything we don't know—or something we think we know but want to make sure we're right about—we just wander into the Bee Pee Ell.

> **The society of Boston was and is quite civilized, but refined beyond the point of civilization.**
> **—T. S. Eliot**

We're not sure what Tom Eliot was saying, but we understand what he meant. We've never let civilization get in the way of refinement around here. We thought Isabella Stewart Gardner (Mrs. Jack to us) was a little odd, building a Florentine palazzo on the edge of the Fenway muck, swilling beer, and walking down Tremont Street with a lion cub on a leash. But the woman had refinement, and when she passed on we turned her palazzo into a museum and named it after her.

And it's not like we needed any more museums. Harvard has so many that they're thinking of crating up a couple and shipping them off to Goodwill. And the Em Eff Ay has been chockablock with stuff for decades now.

The Em Eff Ay, of course, is how we pronounce the MFA—the Museum of Fine Arts on Huntington Avenue.

OF COURSE, THE MFA DOES OCCASIONALLY OFFER 'CUTTING EDGE' EXHIBITS

MUSEUM OF FINE ARTS

RED SOX BASEBALL CARDS

FROM THE BEN AFFLECK COLLECTION

It's the one with the green Indian on horseback out front. The Em Eff Ay is sort of Boston's attic—it has paintings of Sam Adams, tankards made by Paul Revere, that sort of thing. But it also has rooms filled with ahtwork from ancient Greece and Rome and Egypt, from England and France and Italy, from all over Asia.

The best thing about the Em Eff Ay is that they never throw anything away. They may move things around once in a while, like when the Monet people send over a few dozen paintings of water lilies for a few months. And they may not always know where the stuff comes from—it's impolite to inquire whether the Nazis might have stolen it. But they have so many *objets d'art* by now that they wouldn't know what to do with anything by Andy Warhol anyway. You want modern, you go to Noo Yawk.

Thank God the Boston critics don't like me. If they did I should feel I was hopeless.
—Isadora Duncan

We liked Isadora's dancing all right. We just couldn't stand those interminable damned speeches about Maxim Gorky and the color red and the untrammeled progress of the soul. That's why Mayah Curley banned her from the stage. It wasn't that breast-baring business—everybody already had nodded off. If we want sermonizing, we'll go to King's Chapel or dial up Dr. Silber.

We love dancing. We go to the *Nutcracker* every December. We love the performing arts. That's how Boston got to be a tryout town for New York. If a show couldn't survive our discerning eye, it wouldn't stand a chance on the Great White Way.

That's why producers finally made New York a tryout town for us. If *Cats* and *Phantom* and *Les Miz* run for four or five years on Broadway, they've got a decent chance of making it at the Wang or the Colonial or the Shubert. Andrew Lloyd Webber knows enough not to bring a weak book anywhere near Tremont Street. We'd close him in three days, before the *Phoenix* even got to review him.

So we don't get a lot of new theater anymore. That doesn't mean we're some kind of touring-company backwater. We're just unbending in our aesthetic judgment, timeless in our taste. Just wait 'till they bring *Miss Saigon* around again. The lines will stretch all the way down to the Common.

And just because we didn't like Brahms's *Second* doesn't mean we don't know our music. We started a Handel and Haydn society in 1815, when the rest of the world thought they were a Hessian law firm. The Bee Ess Oh has been around since 1881, and we've never had to give away tickets over the radio.

Ah, kulcha

We can hum the "1812 Overture" (complete with howitzer) from memory, we've got streets named after Mendelssohn and Liszt, and we knew Lenny Bernstein when he was a sixie at Latin.

That doesn't make us a bunch of stiff-backed highbrows, though. When the weather warms up, we put a bunch of tables on the Symphony Hall floor and uncork champagne. Or we spread blankets at the Esplanade down by the Rivah and listen to the Pops for free on the 4th of July.

We're on the orchestral cutting edge here. Arthur Fiedler wore a Beatles wig when he conducted *A Hard Day's Night.* John Williams was waving his baton for us back in his early *Star Wars* days. We've had seminal rockers, too. Remember Freddie "Boom-Boom" Cannon? Barry and the Remains? Moulty and the Barbarians?

We even had something called the Boston Sound for about three weeks in the seventies—and that's not counting the group Boston, which had a monster album called *Boston. Boston* went platinum. What did Brahms's *Second* ever do?

Boston's three major industries are sports, politics and revenge.
—Larry Moulter

Back in 1986, when we made it to the World Series and the Super Bowl, and the Celts won another (can you count to 16?) world title, Boston was the sporting Hub of the Universe. The Mayah hung a banner from City Hall that said so. Not that we needed banners to remind us. We have more than we've got room for, anyway.

We have The Marathon (everybody else has a 26-mile footrace). We have the Head of the Charles, the biggest boat race anywhere. We have the Yale game. We have the Sox, the country's longest-running soap opera. What else do we need?

We already have one of everything. You can't start a league without a Boston team in it. In fact, we have so many teams in so many leagues that we don't mind losing one every so often. The Washington Redskins used to be here. So did the Atlanta Braves. The Patriots said they were leaving for Hahtfid. We said, "So?" They'd left for Foxborough a million years ago, and Foxborough's practically a suburb of New York.

Besides, we still have the Sox, the Celts, and the Bruins, and they've been here as long as Faneuil Hall. Our great-grandfathers saw Babe Ruth pitch in Fenway. They watched the Bruins skate in the Gahden back when they cleaned the ice with shovels. Most of us grew up watching Cooz dribbling on the parquet.

No doubt, we got spoiled. We were always carrying Jim Lonborg off the Fenway mound, Bobby Orr was always scoring Cup-winning goals in midair, and John Havlicek was always stealing the ball. Okay, for fifteen years or so, we rested on our laurels, even while they were decomposing.

The nineties weren't the most exuberant sporting times around here. Those t-shirts that said "Harvard Football, Team of the '90s" referred to the 1890s. Then the Patsies won three Super Bowls, and the Sawx beat the Cardinals (not to be confused with the Cahdnal) for the Series, and we were back on top of the world. Not that we ever cared much about it, of course. When you're the Hub of the Universe, our planet is merely a dusty corner.

Ah, kulcha

How we know yiz ahnt from heah

- You call it the Museum of Fine Arts.
- You call it the Boston Marathon.
- You never saw the Pats play in Boston.
- You take a tour of Harvard Yard.
- You don't remember Arthur Fiedler.

Names and numbiz

There are not ten men in Boston equal to Shakespeare.
—unknown Bostonian, 1891

This isn't a city, remember. This is a town. So we know who you are, unless we couldn't care less who you are. Which means that we'll rarely call you by your full name, unless we work for the IRS. And the only time we'll ask you for your full name is if we're swearing you in or checking your claim against the Unclaimed Money List. We've been eating broiled scrod at Jimmy's forever, but there aren't a hundred Bostonians who know that his last name was Doulos.

One name will suffice. We know you by your first name. Or we know you by your last name or an abbreviation thereof. Or we know you by your nickname. Or we know you by your title. Or we know you by your number.

We know you by your first name if you've been here so long that you're damned near unavoidable or if we've seen you on TV so often that we set you a dinner plate. Like Eliot and Barry.

We know you by your last name if you insist (Silber) or if there's only one of you (Belichick). If we can't spell you (Yastrzemski), we'll abbreviate you (Yaz).

We know you by your nickname if it's stylish (Dapper) or if your first name doesn't fit you (Duane).

We know you by your title if there's always one of you (Cahdnal) and if there's only one of you at a time (Mayah).

We know you by your number (4) if you played so long and so well at Fenway or the Garden that they hung your Arabic numeral from the rafters or glued it to the right-field fence.

By first name

Natalie
Ms. Jacobson, still TV's favorite talking head. When she and former hubby Chet Curtis read the news together, they were the Ozzie-and-Harriet of the local airwaves. Because easygoing Bill Weld was nicer to Natalie, he beat the irascible Doctah Silbah for the Guvnah's chair.

Eliot and Barry
Ubiquitous sofa siblings who invented "shoppertainment" and furnished every love nest in the region with everything from mattresses to ahmwahz. They've been doing their radio and TV ads for Jordan's Furniture (not to be confused with Jordan Marsh) for decades, but nobody knows their last name. It's Tatelman.

Keith
Inheritor of the Pops baton once wielded by founder Ahthah Fiedlah. Boyish looks keep Mr. Lockhaht preserved permanently at 35. Now a perennial summer seasonal, like buttah-and-shugah con.

Kevin
Kevin Hagan White, former Mayah of America. Master builder of downtown. Loner in love with his city. Operated without desk and without portfolio. Transformed cobwebbed Parkman House into chic political salon. Coulda been Jimmy Carter's veep if Teddy hadn't turned thumbs down.

Larry

Larry (not Lawrence) Joe Bird, retired Celtics immortal. Self-styled Big Hick from French Lick who relocated to Causeway Street and wore green exclusively for 13 years. Hobnobbed with artistic rivals Magic and Michael. Called by last name only by Johnny Most, former Seltz radio announcer.

Ray

Raymond Leo Flynn, former Mayah, Vatican ambassador and Celtics draftee. Was usually glimpsed jogging through the naybahoods and chatting up The People. The man most likely to be quaffing a Harp lager and singing "Wild Colonial Boy" on the adjacent barstool at J. J. Foley's. Shaped Bill Clinton's urban policies; was Pontiff's roving planetary troubleshooter.

Ming

Mr. Tsai, the Blue Ginger Man who fused East and West in his televised kitchen. Foodies from Connecticut to California line up outside his Wellesley restaurant to gobble his signature sea bass. Not to be confused with brother Ming Tsai, who frequently impersonates him to snag scarce reservations elsewhere.

Nomar

We were on a first-name basis with the former Sox shortstop from day one because we would have had to say "ah" too many times if we'd called him Gahshuhpah-rah. For eight years, we implored Nomah to hit a homah, and he obliged often enough that he'll probably be going to the Hall of Fame. When he decamped for Chicago, it was a regional day of mourning. No moah Nomah.

Teddy

Edward Moore Kennedy, Senator-for-life. If his name were Edward Moore, a man named McCormack once said, his candidacy would have been a joke. Has succeeded Strom Thurmond as upper-chamber dean. Deeply spiritual, was a regular at midnight Mass on the Vinyid.

TEDDY

Roger

Roger Clemens, former Sox hurler. Pronounced Rawjuh. Once the hero of the Fenway bleacherites, who saluted him with Bronx cheer when he donned Yankee pinstripes.

Tip

The late Thomas P. O'Neill, Jr., former House Speekah in Washington. Cigar-chomping backslapper and backroom raconteur who could croon "Apple Blossom Time" in his sleep. Known for aphorism "All politics is local," but trotted globe on fact-finding missions, brandishing pitching wedge. Son Thomas P. O'Neill, III, was known as "Tip-squeak."

By last name

Belichick

His birth certificate says William, but we wouldn't dare be that familiar. Once he won a few Super Bowl rings, we were tempted to genuflect. It'd be nice if he were a bit more chatty, but he is what he is, and nobody's complaining. If he wears that hooded grey sweatshirt any longer, it'll be museum quality—like the Shroud of Turin.

Brady

Tom Terrific, the quarterback who led the former Patsies to a bunch of Soopah Bowl triumphs. Boyish charm has attracted a huddleful of matronly groupies who'd love to mother him. Too bad he has to wear his helmet to work.

Curley

Known as James Michael Curley during reign as Mayah, but subsequent immortality required mere surname. Subject of semibiographical *Last Hurrah*. Was the Purple Shamrock, name now borne by tavern across the street from twin Curley statues (standing and sitting). Traditional mayoral license plate (576) taken from number of letters in full name. Recovery of his missing desk most significant find since Dead Sea scrolls.

BULJAH

Bulger
William M., the former Senate and UMass president. Pronounced Buljah in native South Boston and elsewhere. Noted epigrammarian and peruser of Greek classics. Occasional reader of the *Boston Globe*, which he regards as suburban daily.

Jacobs
He owns the Broons and the building, but he lives in Buffalo, and he's not much for hanging out at Quincy Market. We always lumped him in with the rest of the Jacobs Brothers (how many were there, anyway? Two? Three? More?) and thought he was Jewish. Turns out he's Catholic, baptized Jeremy. Who knew? Maybe if he gave us a break on the Bud Lite and the peanuts, we'd call him Jerry.

Kerry

John Forbes Kerry, who'll be our junior senator until he's a senior citizen or until he's elected President. Kennedy may be Teddy but Kerry is Kerry. Early on, he was encouraging the JFK thing as a sort of Camelot carryover, but nobody bought it. Maybe it's because he went to Yale.

KERRY

Silber

Dr. John, former Bee Yew president-for-life and erstwhile candidate for Guvnah. Known for relaxed demeanor except when provoked by Natalie or a certain orange-haired WASP sonovabitch. Known as Doctor for philosophical, not surgical, qualifications.

By abbreviated last name

Cooz
Bob Cousy, Seltz playmaker/prestidigitator. Memorized and avoided all 389 dead spots on Garden parquet floor. Famous for blind passes to startled mates. Only person other than parents to refer to Red Auerbach as "Arnold." "WE LOVE YA, COOZ" from human bullhorn in second balcony on retirement day made him weep.

Yaz
Carl Yastrzemski, unspellable Sox icon. Nobody ever could remember whether the "s" or "z" came first. Box scores identified him as Ystrmski. Tabloid headlines truncated him early in career.

YAZ PICKS SOX TO COP FLAG

was perennial spring harbinger. The vigil for his 3,000th base hit was longest wait since Godot.

By nickname

Dapper
Albert L. O'Neil, former city councilor. Not to be confused with the late Tip O'Neill or any of his progeny. Was the public official most likely to whisper a Hail Mary over your casket—or pull you off the road, waving a revolver and invoking a citizen's arrest. Acquired nickname during the 1940s, for reasons now unclear. Last glimpsed still chasing skirts in Rozzie.

Red
Arnold Auerbach, former Celtics coach. Stress of winning perennial world championships on uneven parquet

floor turned his russet locks to white. Famed for igniting cigar on bench when victory appeared inevitable. Is frozen in that pose in sculpture at Quincy Market.

Tuna
Duane William Parcells, former Patriots and Jets coach, now rustling beef on the hoof in Dallas. Bears passing resemblance to actual chicken of the sea. "You guys must think I'm Charlie Tuna," he once said to players after failed attempt to gull him. Said to prefer Tuna to Duane.

Whitey
James Bulger, reputed mobster and FBI operative. Brother of (and not to be confused with) the former Senate and UMass president. Has white hair, usually covered by a Sox cap. Whereabouts unknown, but said to be residing in the Bahamas, the Republic of Ireland, Thailand, South Boston, or all of the above.

By title

The Cahdnal

If he issues an ecclesiastical edict, the radio will call him Sean Cardinal O'Malley, just to be official about it. Otherwise, he's just the Cahdnal. If you don't know who he is, it won't make any difference anyway. For folks of a certain age, the Cahdnal still means Cushing.

The Guvnah

Bill Weld, who held the job for about ten minutes, tried to convince us that we had co-governors for eight years (remember Welducci?), but we weren't having it. There's only one guy in the corner office. It's His (or Her) Excellency—the Guvnah—and he's usually a Republican who's already dying of boredom by the time he's finished raising his right hand.

UNTAPPED ENERGY SOURCE...

STATEHOUSE

GUSTS OF HOT AIR

BEACON HILL

WIND-MILL

The Speekah

Mistahspeekah to you. When Tip was ambling around Capitol Hill, he was The Speekah. Now, and usually, it's the man who wields the House gavel on Beacon Hill. Is addressed as Mistahspeekah by the members even when absent.

Names and numbiz

The Mayah

Hosanna to Hizzonah. If he's been around for a couple of terms, we'll call him (and he's always a he) by his first name—e.g., Kevin, Ray. We usually don't call Mayah Menino Tom because people might think we're talking about the Patriots quarterback. And we'll never call him Mumbles—at least not to Hizzoner's face.

MAYAH
MENINO

By number

4

"Bawstin goal scored by Numbah Foah—Oah." Back when we knew what the Stanley Cup looked like, it was Bobby Orr and the Big Bad Broons. When they traded him to Chicago, it was as if we'd sent the Custom House to the Loop.

7

Phil Esposito, the golden-handed Bruin ("Jesus saves, but Espo scores on the rebound") wore it first. Ray Bourque, who was team captain for so long that it became his first name (Captain Ray Bourque) inherited the numeral. When it came time to raise Espo's number to the Gahden rafters, Bourque literally gave him the shirt off his back and rolled another 7. (See below.)

8

The man they call Yaz. Everybody from Cleary Square to Orient Heights could imitate his batting stance. He owned the number so completely that nobody remembers who wore it before him.

9

The Splendid Splinter. When he went off to war, the Sox kept his number in cold storage. Now, Route 9 is called Ted Williams Highway. Roughly 700,000 people claim to have seen him homer in his last at-bat. Though he's been decapitated and cryogenically preserved, Teddy Ballgame still figures to hit .300 when he returns.

33

Why did Larry Bird wear a rookie's number? Because it was symmetrical, and because the Celtics already had retired everything else. A generation of roundballers grew up wearing twin 3s, sporting a rat-tail and wiping sweaty palms on their sneaker soles.

77
As a consolation prize for giving his number back to the aforementioned Mr. Esposito, Ray Bourque wore 77 until it also went up to the rafters. When the Captain's kid plays for the Bruins, he'll have to wear 777.

How we know yiz ahnt from heah
• You call the Cahdnal by his last name.
• You think Dapper is Tip's brother.
• You think Curley was one of the Stooges.
• You recognize Jerry Jacobs on the street.
• You don't remember Kevin.

Our back pages

Boston commits the scholastic error and tries to remember too much.
—H. G. Wells

We're the second chapter in every history book in every school from Maine to California, right after Plymouth Rock and John Alden and Squanto. We're the Boston Massacre and the Tea Party and Paul Revere's ride and the whites of their eyes, et cetera.

They'll rock you in our cradle of liberty until you're damned near catatonic. The problem is, the story always ends with John Hancock writ large in Philadelphia. They never get around to Ponzi or Rosie Ruiz or Billy Buck.

Everyone knows about the San Francisco earthquake and the Chicago fire and the Oklahoma dust bowl and the Johnstown flood. But how about the Boston Molasses Flood? Here's what they never teach you about our town in your school—and what they left out.

Boston is founded (1630)

Bill Blackstone had the neighbors over for a drink—and inadvertently founded Boston. The "Hermit of Shawmut" lived by himself on Beacon Hill, reading his books, drinking from a spring, munching apples, and riding his saddled bull along the shore. When John Winthrop and his fellow campers discovered that the Charlestown water was wretched, Blackstone invited them over to imbibe. They ended up buying most of his land and building a city around him. "Was there not room enough for all of ye?" Blackstone groaned. "Could ye not leave the hermit in his corner?"

Boston's "Mohawks" brew up saltwater tea (1773)

Their password was "Me Know You," but even their own mothers wouldn't have known them. If the British occupiers had recognized the Sons of Liberty who were hosting the infamous Tea Party ("That you under that blanket, Mr. Hancock?"), they would have strung them up on the Common. So the rebels wore tattered clothes, smeared their faces with soot and grease, carried homemade tomahawks and grunted "ugh-ugh" all the way to Griffin Wharf. It was the last decent thing Bostonians dumped in the harbor before they put in a sewage system.

The Irish and Yankees begin the beguine (1837)

A Yankee bucket brigade was quickstepping toward a domestic conflagration. An Irish funeral procession was inching toward the graveyard. Broad Street wasn't nearly broad enough to accommodate both groups, so they danced a contentious *pas de deux* in mid-thoroughfare. While the coffin sat abandoned on a side street and the flames spread roofward, the firemen and mourners had at each other with cobblestones and staves, then repaired to local taprooms to rehydrate. The city fathers subsequently decided that a professional fire department might be a good idea.

Doc Morton knocks himself out to end pain (1846)

William Morton was playing around with his dog and a bottle of ether, experimenting with painless tooth extraction. The dog, who didn't care to have his canines yanked, smashed the bottle. Morton soaked up the spillage with a handkerchief, gave it a good snort, and slipped off to visit Morpheus. "Gentlemen, this is no humbug," said a surgeon at Mass General after removing an anesthetized patient's jaw tumor. "This is the main advantage of ether," Dr. Hunter S. Thompson concluded in 1971, after a bit of recreational research. "It makes you behave like the village drunkard in some early Irish novel."

The great fire (1872)

We didn't need a cow to kick over a lantern. Just a spark in a wooden elevator shaft in a dry-goods building filled with hoop skirts, corsets, and bustles. With the fire horses down sick, the water pipes rusted, and the hydrants defective, 763 buildings stuffed with wool, leather, paper, and cotton were reduced to rubble and cinders. It was urban renewal, Boston-style.

Bell stumbles upon the telephone (1876)

Alexander Graham Bell had been fiddling with something called a harmonic telegraph in his attic workshop on Exeter Place, trying to improve upon what Sam Morse had wrought. No go. So he rigged up a whatzit from a crude mouthpiece, a brass pipe, a platinum needle, and a container of sulfuric acid. While noodling around, Bell spilled acid on his tweed trousers and shouted to his assistant in the adjacent room: "Mr. Watson, come here, I want to see you!" The assistant heard, clear as a Bell. Watson put him on hold, then dialed *69.

The Great Molasses Flood (1919)

It wasn't a joke to the twenty-one souls who drowned in it or to the DPW, which had to sop up two-and-a-half million gallons of the stuff. When a giant iron tank exploded on a January afternoon, a sea of molasses rolled through the North End, smashing half-a-dozen buildings, smothering a score of horses, and sending five-dozen people to the morgue or the hospital. That's why we don't talk about anything being as slow as molasses in January around here any more. Even now on a muggy day, they say, you still can sniff a faint, sweet, and sticky whiff along Commercial Street.

Ponzi builds pyramid from stamps (1920)

Pyramid schemes had been around since Cleopatra. The last ones in pay off the first ones out; you do the math. But Charles Ponzi found a way to make the numbers seem real. He trafficked in "international reply coupons," which could be turned in for foreign postage stamps, and profited on the difference in exchange rates. He promised investors a 50 percent return. When his $7 million pyramid collapsed in a matter of months, Ponzi went to jail, where he bred white mice.

The Sox trade the Babe to the Yankees (1920)

Harry Frazee was desperate for cash. He'd had several Broadway flops, was trying to get *No, No, Nanette* on the stage, and owed money to the men who'd sold him the ball club and the ballpark. So Frazee borrowed $500,000 from New York owner Jacob Ruppert. All he had to give in return was a mortgage on Fenway and one George Herman Ruth.

"You're going to ruin yourself and the Red Sox in Boston for a long time to come," manager Ed Barrow warned Frazee. The Yankees won seven world championships with the Big Fellow. The Town Team didn't win another until 2004. It was, the *Globe's* Dan Shaughnessy wrote, the "Curse of the Bambino."

Queen Isadora chides the Philistines (1922)

She had gamboled on the stage at Symphony Hall, draped in a scarlet scarf while cold-roast Boston looked on, stupefied. "You were once wild here," Isadora Duncan reminded the Cabots and Lodges, who'd since been afflicted with cultural constipation. "Don't let them tame you... Look at these statues overhead. They are not real. Knock them down. They are not statues of real Greek gods. I could hardly dance here. Life is not real here." The Brahmin ladies abruptly rose and departed. The Harvard men stood and cheered. The next day, the *Transcript* reported that Duncan had bared a breast. Maybe its correspondent thought he'd been at the Old Howard.

Rosie's (un)run (1980)

She came—literally—out of nowhere, stumbling breathless on trembling legs across the finish line in front of the Pru. Before anyone asked her for ID, Rosie Ruiz already was wreathed and medaled as the

Our back pages

women's winner of the Boston Marathon. "How are you?" inquired Bill Rodgers, the men's champ. "Who are you?" Just another fraud from Noo Yawk who ran all but 26 miles of a 26-mile, 385-yard footrace. "I never saw her," testified Jackie Gareau, later crowned as the true victor. "I beat you once," Ruiz told Gareau the next time they raced. "And I'll beat you again." A quarter-century later, Gareau was honored as the race's Grand Marshal. After alighting from the ceremonial car, she trotted the final 100 meters across the line. "I'm like Rosie now," Gareau realized. "Is this right?"

Billy Buck's bungle (1986)

Everybody woke up great-grandpa and propped the infants in front of the TV set. Saturday night in Shea Stadium and the Town Team was one strike away from finally winning the World Series. Then Steamer throws a wild pitch (or was it a passed ball?) past Geddy in the tenth, and the game is tied. Mookie Wilson taps a bleeder, which bounces, bounces, then doesn't bounce, and rolls between Bill Buckner's legs at first base, and the Mets escape. "I don't know nothin' about history," Sox manager John McNamara growls, "and I don't want to hear anything about choking or any of that crap." Two nights later, New York wins Game 7—and the Curse of the Bambino continued, until Manny and Johnny and Foulkie and the rest of the Idiots perform an exorcism in St. Louis.

Also by John Powers and Peter Wallace

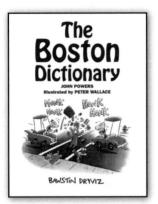

Bostonians, like Texans, Georgians, and the British, have their own version of the English language. This is its Rosetta Stone. Translated by the canny John Powers and illustrated by the uncanny Peter Wallace, here is the book you need: **The Boston Dictionary**.

Natives can brush up on their dialect, if it's been eroded by exposure to too many radio and TV announcers from out of town.

Travelers and newcomers to the Hub of the Universe can learn how to communicate with the indigenous folk.

Passersby really have only two choices: buy this book, or spend a lot of time saying "What?" Samples include:

Dryviz: Cah owniz. "I don't know why everyone says Bawstin dryviz ah so crazy. Evah see a Noo Yawka inside a roedaree? Looks like Uhpawlo 13 in awbit!"

Fawrinnuz: Not from heah. "You can always tell who the fawrinnus ah in Bawstin. They tryda tok to us in English."

Weeuhd: Strange, odd. "I cahn't get ovah how people think we have a weeuhd accent in Bawstin. I mean, we don't even have an accent."

www.oncapepublications.com